A STRATEGY FOR SUCCESS

GOING
BEYOND THE LAW
OF ATTRACTION

A STRATEGY FOR SUCCESS

GOING
BEYOND THE LAW
OF ATTRACTION

MARIANNE HARMS

 iUniverse

A STRATEGY FOR SUCCESS
GOING BEYOND THE LAW OF ATTRACTION

iUniverse books may be ordered through booksellers or by contacting:

iUniverse
1663 Liberty Drive
Bloomington, IN 47403
www.iuniverse.com
1-800-Authors (1-800-288-4677)

Because of the dynamic nature of the Internet, any web addresses or links contained in this book may have changed since publication and may no longer be valid. The views expressed in this work are solely those of the author and do not necessarily reflect the views of the publisher, and the publisher hereby disclaims any responsibility for them.

Any people depicted in stock imagery provided by Thinkstock are models,
and such images are being used for illustrative purposes only.
Certain stock imagery © Thinkstock.

ISBN: 978-1-5320-3243-1 (sc)
ISBN: 978-1-5320-3242-4 (e)

Library of Congress Control Number: 2017913762

Print information available on the last page.

iUniverse rev. date: 10/03/2017

CONTENTS

INTRODUCTION

We can choose to set and achieve our important goals!
We can choose to be successful, happy and prosperous in all our endeavors!
We can choose to pursue our own individual journey in life that we find fulfilling!
We can choose to follow through on all personal commitments!
We can choose to share our life's learning and wisdom with the children!
We can choose to become all that we are capable of becoming!
It's up to us to esteem our life, reach our goals and achieve success!

It will take a belief in our personal value, desire, discipline, and a strategy. Most of all, it will take awareness of what we are doing and where we are going. Somehow awareness, (or consciousness), alone motivates action; however discipline keeps the action going. In every aspect of our lives we will need to use discipline which becomes a part of our daily life when we have awareness *without judgment* of what has gotten in the way of achieving success. Taking right/wrong/good/bad off the table and non-judgmentally considering what is working and what isn't working leads to positive change. These requirements for change will be the focus of what you are about to read. By creating a strategy, a plan of action, and organizing our lives on a daily basis we will maximize the realization of our dreams.

In addition, our attitudes and beliefs about ourselves play a large part in our Self Esteem Level (otherwise called our SEL.) When we see ourselves as unworthy our SEL holds us back from achieving success. Without bringing consciousness to what we think about who we are, our plan of action will lead to frustration and failure as we unconsciously sabotage our best efforts. So as you read this book, keep in mind that being aware of the thoughts we are holding about ourselves, as well as the thoughts about the world in general, and the words we are using to describe them will be the basis for our reality. By following a plan *and* changing our negative attitudes and beliefs we can manifest the successes we wish to create in our lives.

Here's a story; the first of several throughout this book: There I was, standing before a 50' denuded tree. In place of its branches were pegs leading way up to the very top of the tree. At the very top of this very tall tree was a round disk about 18" in diameter. About 5' from the treetop dangled a ring which was fastened to a branch of a nearby tree. My job was to climb 50' up, climb on the disk, leap for the ring, grab a hold of it and finally let go thus being safely lowered to the ground. If I were to miss the ring I would be lowered safely as well. There would be seven such "events" as part of the course. That was the deal with the *Ropes Adventure Course.* Despite the belay harness that I was securely fastened into and despite the seemingly competent belay person on the ground totally responsible for my safety I felt trepidation verging on stark terror. I climbed, stomach doing flips, sweating, shaking, with vomiting a strong possibility. I persevered (as did all 12 fellow adventurers) using all my will and physical strength. As I worked my way on to the disk and stood up the ring loomed before me. I had gotten to the top and now all I had to do was get a hold of the ring... the reward. I leaped—I missed the ring. Taller, shorter, fatter, thinner, younger, older adventurers got the ring—I did not. And I continued to miss it for the next five events. What was going on? About five events into the day the leader explained that the way one approaches the ropes course is the way one approach their life. I thought about that and realized that I often did all the hard work only to miss the reward, achieve the goal, get the ring. At that time in my life it was a startling and truly sad realization. I was struggling in every area of my life and failing miserably. My self esteem was at an all time low and I had the responsibility of supporting and raising two beautiful sons. Keeping body and soul together for them and for myself was a daunting as the 50' tree and I was working damned hard to succeed but success, like the ring, eluded me.

There's a happy ending to the story. We were running out of time that day and only had enough time left for one person to do the last "event". I, like everyone else, was exhausted and I also was feeling hugely discouraged, but stepped into the center and had the harness fastened. Wearily I climbed the tree and stood, once again facing the ring. Each event offered a slightly different challenge yet each was only a variation of the same theme. The current "event" was to climb the tree and work myself around the other side of the tree so that my heels were on the lower pegs and I was holding to the higher pegs directly behind me. This time, I closed my eyes, I let go of judgment, expectations and the outcome. Staying very present to what was happening at the moment, I let go of the pegs and merely leaped with my arms and hands outstretched, fully prepared but relaxed.

I felt the ring in my hands and they firmly closed around it. I hung on joyfully as my fellow adventurers cheered. As I let go and sailed in Peter Pan-like fashion back to terra firma, I got it! I got it! I did the work, let go of outcomes, believed in my own worth, trusted the very right thing would happen, and I succeeded in achieving the goal! Having courage and confidence to live without fear and accomplish goals with strategic planning for attaining one's dreams is what this book is about.

Through understanding the dynamics of our mind and our physical world we can start to use our personal power to create a healthy self-image... that is a sense of our *self*, who we are. A strong self-image radiates, projects and then elicits positive responses from those around us thus reinforcing well-being in mind, body, and spirit.

Mind, body and spirit are three areas of the self that make up the whole of us, who we are....our *self*. How they are managed determines the level of our self esteem which plays itself out in all areas of our lives; relationships, accomplishments, health, satisfaction, and more.

Throughout Part I of this book you will learn about the effects of your SEL, specifically on your social, intimate and spiritual life and how, when lived mindfully, success and joy follow.

In Part II of this book you will be guided to bring your goals to fruition in five steps; deciding what you want, setting your goals, creating a strategic plan, visualizing it in your life, and taking action

Finally, in *Part III*, you will bring your esteemed *self* and your plan of action to a daily awareness. By organizing your day and keeping a record, a journal, of your activity you will stay on track year by year.

Read on….

PART I

ON BECOMING AWESOME

CHAPTER 1

WHAT DOES HIGH SELF-ESTEEM HAVE TO DO WITH SUCCESS?

So how do I love better in a world rampant with fear? It all starts with self love because without it my love is fake, phony. And when I have….well, let's use the word respect instead of love for the moment….when I have self respect my love for others is pure. In fact, it's magnificent. If I can esteem and honor my own existence I can then afford to be selfless. It's a paradox. In order to be selfless, to truly exude authentic love, I have to love me. After all, my *SELF* is all I have to give. I liken it to my home. My home has to be warm and welcoming, it has to smell nice (or at least not smell bad), it has to be comfortable, and most of all safe. It has to be all these things on the *inside* in order to be all these things to visitors from the *outside*.

Furthermore, when I bestow authentic love (or human concern) on my fellow man, I engender trust. There is a felt sense of the genuine caring and from there, the exchange in any relationship, be it intimate, business, friendship, or family, is a win-win. That is success.

So while it may seem that self love is akin to being conceited or self absorbed it is quite the opposite. When we move through life, face its challenges with courage as well as celebrate its successes with joyfulness we are contributing to the evolution of the species. We share life on this planet with all sentient beings and what we bring it depends on our SEL…. Self Esteem Level.

Twelve Traits of People With High SEL:

1. Internal Locus of Control: People either have an internal locus of control, an external locus of control or somewhere in between. What this means is that those with an internal locus of control see themselves as responsible for the outcomes in their lives. Those with an external locus of control view themselves as at the effect external events. So it would be a little like steering a boat through a storm, using all your skills and knowhow, having a solid, sea-worthy boat in the first place, and having all the equipment in working order. Let's say you get through the storm. Someone with an internal locus of control would report that I managed the storm well and chose a good craft, but could have avoided the whole episode if I had checked the weather first. A person with an external locus of control would report, it wasn't

my fault there was a storm but I was lucky (lucky being the operative word) to get through it. It's a matter of being in charge (internal) or a victim (external.)

2. Healthy, mentally and physically: Developing a strong self-esteem promotes both mental and physical health. This is because people who feel good about themselves usually take better care of their body (eat well, exercise, rest, etc.) and take care of their mental well-being by having adequate socialization balanced with solitude in order to deal with stress. They make time for both work and play.

3. Happy: It isn't enough to have people in our life that make us happy. When people have high SEL happiness abides within them. It is not defined by external events and not up for grabs. Although people can't make us happy, they can bring their happiness to us. And while events can bring sadness into our lives, such as a friend dying or an illness in the family, those events don't make us sad people. We are dealing with a sad situation and naturally feel the sorrow around the event. In acknowledging and accepting the feeling of sadness and allowing room for it, there is a sense of peace and with that peace we have an ability to cope.

4. Success: Success, like happiness, is something that people carry in the mind, heart and soul. It is a feeling of being instrumental in bettering their world. It could mean a lot of money or fame, but those are hollow achievements if there is not a sense of accomplishment that leaves one knowing that what they do matters in a most positive way.

5. Ability to assess ourselves and others: Assessing is different than judging in that it is an objective observation devoid of judgment. When I can assess myself in regards to, say, a behavior I can determine whether it works or doesn't work. If I am assessing another person I can make a personal choice as to whether this person resonates with me or shares commonalities and interests. It has nothing to do with the person's worth or value.

6. Boundaries: Everyone needs boundaries. Little children really need and want them. All people need boundaries; couples need them, families need them, co-workers and bosses need them, friends, lovers, and the family dog needs them. Lack of boundaries cause misunderstandings and big, big mistakes. Reading someone's diary can be a big, big mistake and when someone opens someone else's mail without permission, that is crashing a boundary. Having boundaries makes life a lot easier because it tells people about what is acceptable to us, and respecting other's boundaries brings their trust.

7. Identity: People have so many identifications. Their name, their geographic place they call home, work, stature, accomplishments, diseases, etc. Since these can change, identities are relevant to the moment. Today I AM A HANDS ON MOM/DAD, and next year I AM A GRANDPARENT, or I AM A TEACHER (LAWYER, DOCTOR, CUSTODIAN, SOCIALWORKER) and tomorrow I will be A RETIRED TEACHER (LAWYER, DOCTOR, CUSTONIAN, SOCIALWORKER), or I AM A PENNSYLVANIAN but move to CALIFORNIA and now I AM A CALIFORNIAN. I AM THIS, I AM THAT. But what and who am I? What is my identity? Well for a person who has a high SEL they

are in a small way all those things but hold out for the bigger picture knowing they are *all possibilities and potentials* making them simply consciousness personified. I AM MY OWN PROCESS ON MY OWN JOURNEY.

8. Continuity: By definition, it means a consistent flow without interruption. In terms of self-esteem, it refers to the ability to *perform* with general consistency, to *respond* to others in a way that is fairly predictable and acceptable and to *anticipate* with greater or lesser degrees consequences based on choices. Continuity here means fewer surprises. Continuity creates safety.

9. Energetic and positive mirroring: One expression of energetic positive mirroring is to respond to other's experience of an event with positive aliveness which creates an echo effect whereby the level of joy is elevated for all parties involved. Another expression of energetic positive mirroring is to move into the other person's shoes leaving behind personal considerations and be totally present to the other, authentically and compassionately. In either case the mirroring brings all parties into resonance and thereby harmony.

10. Self-confidence: While this may seem to be synonymous with high self-esteem, it differs in that confidence determines how one perceives a task; as a threat or a challenge. In addition, confidence causes one to focus longer on a task, and when there are setbacks to success, confidence enables the person to persevere.

11. Self efficacy: People who have a high SEL hold a belief that they can attain their goals. They believe that through organization and effort they will reach the actualization of an endeavor. It is, basically, the belief in one's ability in a particular area.

12. Body esteem: Taking care of one's body is a result of a high SEL, but *body esteem* is the belief that one is appealing even if the mirror doesn't reflect Madison Avenue ad agency good looks. A person who has facial scarring from a burn may no longer see the scarring because in their estimation of themselves they are appealing based on factors that go beyond any scar.

Imagine the possibility of having all these traits working for us and contributing to our life, our journey through life. So if these are good enough reasons to raise your SEL, read on.

Three Aspects of high SEL:

Social Esteem:
By holding our self in warm regard despite imperfections and limitations we will experience *pride and humility…* instead of *shame and grandiosity.*

By owning our own experiences of thoughts, emotions and sensations and sharing them as our point-of-view we will experience *mindfulness and non-judgment…* instead of *dissociation and perfectionism.*

By having the ability to use depersonalization when attacked and containing our self when provoked by others we will experience *responsiveness and connection*....instead of *reactivity and disengagement.*

By identifying our wants and needs and being responsible for communicating them while holding others to the same we will experience *interdependence and availability*.... instead of *over-dependence and enabling.*

Relational Esteem:

By understanding the dynamics of intimate, committed relationships we will navigate them with more *wisdom and hope...* instead of proceeding in *doubt and despair.*

By holding our relationship in warm regard despite imperfections and limitations we will experience *freedom and relaxed joyfulness...* instead of *control, revenge and/ or resignation.*

By listening until the words we hear are other than our own, speaking our words so they can be heard, and moving from complaint to request, we will experience *connection and resolution...* instead of *disconnection and a power struggle.*

By defining boundaries through the creation of a mutual vision for our relationship we will experience *cooperation and clarity...* instead of *strife and confusion.*

By staying moderate in our partner's rage we will experience *compassion and detachment...* instead of spiraling into *reactivity and revenge.*

Spiritual Esteem:

By remaining faithful in times of disappointment and betrayal we will experience *strength and resilience...* instead of *anger and fear.*

By making daily prayer a part of our life, spontaneously and authentically, in good times and in bad we will *sustain spiritual intimacy and connection with the Divine...* instead of feeling *abandoned and alone.*

By listening with our whole self to what the Divine holds for us creating quiet moments to discern our deepest desire and by being present to those unexpected gifts of grace we will be drawn into *correct action and consolation...* instead of *loss and desolation.*

By knowing our spiritual needs and desire through contemplative mediation and mindfulness we will experience *clarity and encouragement...* instead of *false starts and confusion.*

When we bring our self esteem to the work of setting goals, creating a strategy and organizing our day, we are bound for success. Do the work, let go of the outcome. Success comes in ways unimaginable.

CHAPTER 2

INFLUENCES, DECISIONS, AND CONSEQUENCES

Throughout life we make decisions based on influences to which we are constantly exposed. These influences are sometimes subtle, sometimes fairly obvious. The consequences of decisions you make, based upon influences, can be as much to your advantage as to your disadvantage.

Influences create a sense of what ought to be, based on impressions we get from persons in a position of power. According to *Webster's New World Dictionary,* (Agnes, 2014), it is "...the power of persons or things to affect others, seen only in its effect." SEEN ONLY IN ITS EFFECT is significant when it comes to determining who is running our life. Influence is further defined by Webster as "....the power of a person or a group to produce effects without the exertion of physical force or authority, based only on wealth, social position, ability." The effect is not, therefore, obvious. Influence, by its definition, is subtle, sometimes subliminal, and very potent.

Decisions are judgments we make about ourselves and the world around us, often based on influences. The word "decide" comes from the Latin word "decidra" to cut off. When a decision is reached, alternatives are cut off, no longer considered. Webster defines decisions as a "...judgment or conclusion reached or given." Therefore, a decision, by its definition, is FINAL.

Whenever a decision is reached, a consequence is right behind it. Consequences (Consequantia, in Latin, means to follow) are an upshot, a wake, fallout. Fallout often happens without anything actually being seen or felt. Only if we are aware of the possibility of negative fallout might we look for signs of it and perhaps adjust our decision.

Influences, decisions and consequences: a sequence of power affecting the way we choose to live our life. Three impelling sources of influence that come together to shrewdly weave a fine web into which we unknowingly become caught are the individual, the group and a concentrated collection of groups...the media.

Individual Influence:

Imagine if you will that we are all born with a bucket...a bucket for sand. The bucket represents life and the sand is the stuff of life. Life is complex and complicated so some people may have bigger buckets than others, some may have brand new buckets and other may have used ones...it doesn't matter. At birth, the bucket is empty, leaving us very vulnerable. The sands are the influences that impact us during our life. Everyone has a little sand to put into our bucket and it starts filling up early in life.

Although we are also born with a prevailing sense of self, our frailty is exposed to manipulation, either enhanced or warped by the inevitable "sands" of parental influence that each child experiences from before the moment of birth. As we grow older, we have associations with other individuals who make their contribution; perhaps teachers, clergy, peers, TV heroes and heroines. All sorts of people have an input...some wonderful and some not so wonderful...and since it's unavoidable that's okay. Some contributions are good and some not so good; some are worth keeping and some we keep although we shouldn't. Hopefully we take inventory from time to time and dump the wet heavy sand out, making room for more choice sand.

If we unfortunately allow a lot of misguided people to put a little bit of sand in our bucket over a period of time, we will suddenly find that we have no idea what is in our bucket or why it doesn't feel right. If we allow ourselves the experience of choosing our own sand and the joy of filling our own bucket, a very nice thing happens. All other sand that comes our way merely runs over our bucket, touches us, but does not affect our core, or who we are. It is our bucket and we are at choice.

We are ultimately responsible for sorting through input and either discarding it, or putting it in its proper perspective so as to incorporate it in our worldview. Negative input from others often comes with good intentions, yet may be wrapped up in their own personal fears. Sorting through the influence of others has to do with taking adult responsibility, particularly when it affects how we feel about ourselves.

I frequently see couples who have not taken responsibility for their bucket. She will say, "He makes me feel so inadequate or invisible", or he will say something like that. There comes a time, particularly in an intimate love relationship, whereby each person needs to take responsibility for how they feel about themselves. A more accurate statement would be "I feel so inadequate or invisible" and that is usually true because he or she came into the relationship carrying that image, imposed upon them from individuals in their early childhood, that is now being echoed by their partner. Enough, I say! Dump out that old sand and get to know yourself. If you feel invisible come to know that about yourself and then take the necessary steps, as offered in this book, to create a positive change.

Group Influence:

Successful group influencing is based on the theory that human beings are more comfortable doing what the group does. There is little resistance to following the crowd. The tale of the Hundredth

Monkey as told by Ken Keyes, (Keyes, 1986) illustrates the influential powers of the group. While Keyes recounted the research reports, he took some poetic license in developing the story. Here's Ken's story.

Researchers were doing a study on the Macaca fuscata monkeys on Koshima, a little island off the coast of Japan They dropped sweet potatoes on the beach to see if and how the monkeys would eat them. One of the young monkeys began to wash her sandy sweet potato before she ate it, and eventually taught her family to do likewise.

As time went on, other monkeys of other families also began to wash their sweet potatoes. At the point when 6% of the monkeys on the island were washing their potatoes, all monkeys began to wash their sweet potatoes. It was reported that even the same species of monkeys on other nearby islands also washed their potatoes as well.

The original telling of this research was by Lyall Watson in *Lifetides*, (Watson 1985) There is a discrepancy in the actual research and the result of that discrepancy is to lead Watson's readers to believe some morphogenetic field was responsible for the sudden change in the group. While that is not the case what does come from monkey observation is that there is a generalized group effect among peers (all the young monkeys washed their sweet potatoes whereby the adults may or may not have) and as the older monkeys died the new behavior became the norm. It definitely affected the tribe of monkeys' lives in that the effect of critical mass offered the tribe a now well established alternative giving them more choices regarding water such as bathing, swimming and new foods.

In the book *The Tipping Point,* (Gladwell, *Point*, 2000), author Malcolm Gladwell maintains that there is a tipping point whereby trends to catch on and there is a process that occurs in the evolution of every trend. He describes the process to include three key factors in this evolution; the degree of influence and persuasiveness of the change agent, degree of curiosity and receptivity about the concept or idea, and finally, a felt shift in the environment of a group, community, neighborhood, etc. It takes 6% or 10% (depending on resources) of a population to create a major shift, a critical change.

Groups have more power because critical mass has a sort of collective energy in influencing choices and cultural change. What starts out as a behavior on a personal level that is unique to the individual's experience, through more and more acceptance of that behavior by the group, it becomes an available alternative within the culture. However, as you will learn throughout this book, it takes more than a morphogenetic field effect to create permanent change. It also takes direct communication and group action.

Research has demonstrated that when a certain percentage of a group does a particular thing, it catches on. (See The Journal of Political Economy, Vol. 100, No. 5 (Oct., 1992), pp. 992-1026). Thus, if fads or crazes are reflections of the fashion of the day, most fads have long lost any purpose other than identifying a group. Levi Strauss could not have imagined, even in his wildest dreams, that the tough, heavy duty fabric used for tents and then for work clothes would become a fabric extensively used in the fashion industry. That is a fad that has lasted….most don't.

As we go back over the years, we have seen styles become fads such as western boots, warm-up suits, multiple gold chains, pierced noses, tattoos, knee socks, ankle bracelets, inch long nails, skinny eyebrows, bushy eyebrows, crinoline skirts, poodle skirts, mini skirts, maxi skirts, the bob, the bun etc. all of which had a specific function and still do, prior to becoming a fad. But fads come and go, they peak and wane.

I feel a story coming on. When I was in eighth grade Buddy Herman came to school wearing white socks. Buddy was popular… a leader of sorts and way out of my league. Well everyone noticed his white socks and there was a lot of finger pointing and a chanting "Buddy's wearing white socks, Buddy's wearing white socks." Buddy nipped it in the bud. He said, "Hey, this is what's happening in high school. All the guys are wearing white socks" which wasn't true because my sister was in high school and she said so. Probably his mother bought him white socks, end of story. Needless to say, a few kids came to school that week with white socks and before you could say Jack Robinson all the "in" guys were wearing white socks. That was a fad happening right before my eyes. Did it last? I have no idea. I moved and went to Catholic school where everyone wore white socks as part of a uniform. What about uniforms? It creates an instant group identity.

Fads and group cohesiveness can be interesting, fun and usually harmless. When group influences push you to carry out unhealthy choices it can often lead to regret. Later in this book you will read more about mindless choices driven by influences that we are not aware of, influences that take us off our path. Individuality! It is the expression of the *self* that becomes lost when we follow the crowd mindlessly. It is the well-established sense of the *self* that can transcend the power of collective influence.

Media's Influence:

As you peruse a fashion magazine, perhaps one for which you paid $10 or $15, notice that a generous three quarters of it is a catalog of advertisers selling fantasies and dreams that come in bottles, tubes or jars…that can be raced on pristine courses…worn on the ears, neck, hands or a very muscular back…or played with like an expensive toy. The selling tool is youth, sex, beauty and wealth. Dreams of wealth, luxury, glamour and Eros are delivered to you with tremendous impact and with a sense of authority.

It is interesting to note that the majority of media companies in 1983 in America were owned by only 50 powerful corporations. According to *The New Media Monopoly*, (Bagdikin, 2004), that number went down to 24 in 1992 and in 2000 the number of corporations running media is 5, maybe 6. This is a sort of central intelligence that determines the people's truths and realities. In addition, these media corporations are linked with other industries through common financial interests all of whom have the ultimate motivation to impose a mighty influence on this society for profit. And, collectively, members of this society will accept these corporate truths as fact without regard to the well-being of the individual.

The message, created through the genius of Madison Avenue advertising agencies, backed by multibillion dollar advertising budgets, is that glamour and luxury happen to beautiful people and to be beautiful is to have all of the above. This forceful barrage of ideas directed by media to the public is partly responsible for some of our misguided values and misdirected attitudes. It stands to reason, therefore, that with genius and dollars churning out tons of copy, we *will* get the message. Allowing ourselves to get caught up in the momentum of advertising can prevent us from seeing the real beauty in our life. Frozen images, airbrushed and arranged, become the yardstick with which we measure our own reality. A sense of urgency is attached to the insatiable desire to replicate the impossible dream.

CHAPTER 3

THE UNFOLDING *"SELF"*

A good question at this point would be; how did I reach the SEL I am currently at? Whether we have a high SEL or a low one, we, most likely, did not achieve it consciously. Influences, your decisions based on those influences and the consequences happened to us while we were "asleep at the wheel". From about birth on, (although some researchers believe there is a lot going on brain-wise in the latter part of the last trimester of pregnancy), the infant's brain begins to make sense of the world he is entering merely based on feedback. There's not a whole lot of analyzing and logic in this wee little brain. In Chapter one you were introduced to the notion that we are all born into the world with a bucket which is filled with sand. That is, our bucket is filled with *other people's* sand. The cause of this dilemma has to do with growing up in an adult world.

Developmentally speaking, the infant's first growing up task in life is to adjust to separation from the mother's womb. That happens at birth and rather rudely in some cases. Imagine coming down the birth canal, leaving behind a world of warm, buoyant fluid. Normally, nutrition is provided for so completely and effortlessly "room service" pales in comparison. Getting adequate oxygen is also effortless. In this world there is serene darkness and the gentle thump, thump, thump of a heart; a consistent reminder that all is well. In fact, all sounds this little human being hears are familiar, muted, and gentle. Enter now into a brightly lit, dry, noisy world of gravity where after being smacked and aspirated (ok, they no longer smack, but they did to most of us over 60) this baby fills its lungs for the first time. Ouch! The birth canal is narrow and to pass through it takes this child's best efforts as well as its mother's. But finally the journey is complete and this child is now an Earthling. As soon as baby finds its way from the mother's belly to her breast where, laying warmly on her heart and in her arms, he beings to instinctively suckle. Mother and infant are accomplishing the first task of "bonding." Life is good and baby can begin to thrive. But birthing doesn't always go so smoothly. Sometimes baby comes too early and rather than hearing the mother's heartbeat and feeling her warm arms all baby experiences is a warm receiving blanket and a lot of tubes in an incubator, not mom's arms. Better than the alternative, incubators are no substitute for mom. Sometimes baby comes at exactly the right time but the mother is too ill or unprepared to nurture this child. There are other reasons why the bond between mother and infant can be thwarted but infants who are eventually held securely and attended to lovingly develop a sense of trust and safety. Erik H. Erikson, in *Identity: Youth and Crisis,* (Erikson, 1968), places as much if not more importance on the completion of this developmental task than on subsequent tasks and describes it as the development of trust vs. mistrust.

The ability of the child to experience the mother as consistently available and warm enables the child to move on to the next stage fully prepared to complete that task. Without it, the child struggles onward.

The second task that rears its daunting challenge is the exploration of the child's world. This occurs when the child begins to crawl and walk. Exploring one's world at this age can be exciting, or terrifying, or not-at-all. The child that leaves her mother's or father's leg and wanders off around a corner quickly scurries back to relocate the parent. If this is successfully done enough times the child learns "object permanence" by leaving the object (i.e. mother or father) and returning to check-in, if you will. Although the concept initially introduced by child psychologist and researcher Jean Piaget has been challenged, it implies that during this developmental stage a child believes that if dad or mom or anyone else is not visible, they do not exist. This coming and going is called rapprochement and during this stage of exploration the child develops the ability to go from sight of, say mom, and yet understand that she still exists. With a firm grasp on object permanence the child can begin to explore the ins and outs of its world. With proper supervision this is done safely. Sometimes however, mothers and fathers of eight or ten children miss a few ins and outs and the child gets injured… not safe. Or lost… also not safe. Did you ever hear the cry of a child lost in the supermarket? It isn't pleasant because you hear the terror in the child's cry. On the other hand, sometimes mothers and fathers are overprotective and all the child hears is "No, don't touch that" or "No, stay here by me" or "No, you'll get hurt or dirty." "No, be careful!" "No, No, No!" "Me do" is met with "No, I'll do it." This little person has no idea of its world except through the lens of the parents. Basically, it's not safe because there is a sense of "warning" around each exploration. When this stage is completed successfully the child has a sense of autonomy. Unsuccessfully, the child experiences internalized fear, going about an insecure world.

At about the age of four or five the child begins to form an identity. They now have playmates, often playing with their siblings. They learn to pretend and develop imaginations. The task of this developmental stage is to initiate roles and explore their gender.

Here comes a story! My grandson provides a terrific example of this task. He was really good at playing his part and I was fair-to-pretty good. Here's what happened. When he was about five years old he came into the kitchen where his father was preparing dinner. He had a dishtowel tied around his neck and with arms akimbo announced that he was Batman. "Batman, said I, you look just like Batman." "Oh no, Grandma, I AM Batman" and with that his mother indicated with a nod and a look, that I might just agree if I wanted to be in good with him. "Well, Batman, I've never had dinner with you so would you sit next to me at the table?" With that my grandson puffed his chest out and gave me the biggest smile. So this is an example of a child's imagination creating his identity. The point is, when a child receives validation of his or her imagined role at this age they can safely try on other roles. If, in this example, I were to say to my grandson, "Go take that towel off Levi and come eat dinner" or on the contrary, "You ARE Batman. Let's go get you a cape and that mask he wears and let's buy some comic books so you can talk like Batman. You can be Batman, but you'll be my kind of Batman", he would possibly have given up his imaginary roles and be invisible or would have become all too visible (pushy). Either way, expressing identity would not be safe.

Assignment of developmental tasks to developmental life stages from infancy to babyhood, on to childhood, adolescence, young adulthood, middle-age, older and old-old age serves as a framework for the unfolding of all individuals. It is a progression of the unfolding self. It is important to add here however that the particular essence that is distinctively yours, that which your come into the world with, be it shy, outgoing, introspective, carefree determines how others respond to us and how we respond to the "sand" that others have put in our bucket.

From the moment others laid eyes our tiny infant self, our essence was responded to. The doctor or midwife, mom, dad, grandparents uncles, aunts, sister, brother, all had word to describe us. But it wasn't the words, it was the feelings and energy behind the words that affected our essence. "He's a little precious" has a very different feeling to it than, "wow, you're going to have your hands full". That essence plays itself out in the hospital nursery with one baby sleeping peacefully, the other crying incessantly, while one other baby is busy looking around. There is the ever-hungry baby and the baby that could take the nipple or leave it and then the one who wants to suckle but gets too excited. Some babies are easily disturbed and others can be calm through upending events. Babies are different, they, each one, have their own essence.

As a result of this reinforcement of our essence the child develops a personality. A personality is a distortion to greater or lesser degrees of our early essence. It is a response to the response. Personalities are therefore expressed, and then responded to by others. Our attitudes are developed as a result of feedback to our personality and lifestyles are incorporated to support those attitudes. Again, to greater or lesser degrees these work in our best interest. The presentational self comes into action as a mask or defense against shame or doubt as to our okay-ness. Our innate essence, ensuing personality, our attitudes, lifestyle choices and presentational self is an unfolding process of "becoming" who we believe we are. Based on the responses to our early essence and the success, or lack thereof, of the tasks of developmental stages throughout childhood we learn to experience ourselves, our world and others through the lenses of those inputs. Most people grow away from their true self.

Because parenting is never perfect most if not all children suffer a disturbance to their core energy between the ages of 0 to 7. All a child can do about that disturbance is to develop a strong defense around it. That said, the task of adulthood is to make the necessary adjustments to our SEL in order to experience life fully and become passionately alive.

We respond to inadequate or inappropriate attention as little children with personal dramas. That could be temper tantrums, withdrawing, threatening bodily harm, misbehaving, and other acting-out behaviors. It is our defense.

Every significant detail of how we were talked to, touched, what we were taught as well as the physical, emotional and mental attributes of our parents are recorded in our brains and becomes hardwired into our subconscious from where we derive our view of the world as either safe or dangerous.

Most parents have every intention to provide love and safety for their infants but when that doesn't happen, it is more a function of the fears and misgivings of the parent than the child's lack of worthiness. Of course little children don't see it that way. Little children believe they are all powerful and when they experience their world as dangerous they believe they are at fault. That perpetuates the dysfunction. It is only in waking up to this discrepancy or misunderstanding that future generations are willing to meet the challenge that evolution is calling us to, actually begging us to. That is to end the generational legacy of family dysfunction played out in our personal dramas. If each generation fails to meet this challenge the species does not evolve. Why might this be important? The Earth needs its inhabitants, (that would be us), to evolve so that we don't destroy it. There is a bit of urgency to this calling. If each generation didn't take on the job of growth evolution would slow down, stop, then reverse and we would regress.

So, why it that important to us as individuals living here on Planet Earth? It's about getting past our personal dramas so that we have the freedom to make wise and appropriate choices for ourselves and to cooperate with the rest of humanity on this journey to self completion.

As our true self continues to unfold we, as adults, can now make conscious choices. The opposite of making conscious choices is to react. We now view our self and our world in a healthy way and to respond rather than react. Reactivity keeps us in old habits and stepping out of old habits opens up a new and positive experience. After all, life gives back to us what we put in. If we're asleep to the pain, life will simply let us stay in the pain. If we wake up and make healthy choices, life responds to us in kind.

CHOICES BASED ON LOVE	**CHOICES BASED ON FEAR**
LOVE	**FEAR**
We are aware of what we are thinking, doing and being.	We sleep walk.
We remain objective in our responses to events.	We have knee jerk reactivity to events.
We foster life by being creative.	We destroy possibilities before they have a chance to manifest.
We take responsibility for the outcomes of our successes and failures.	We shirk our duties, put blame on factors outside ourselves and yet carry guilt.
We appreciate our gifts and talents and those of others that are different than ours.	We criticize and fear others that are unlike ourselves.
We risk being who we are authentically regardless of other's judgments.	We are disingenuous to gain approval.
We have self respect and hold others in respect at all times.	We invade other's boundaries.
We communicate by listening and being fully present to another.	We only hear our own agenda while communicating with another.
We say what we mean and we mean what we say, after giving it due thought.	We lie in order to escape our own truth when we feel it to be unacceptable.

CHAPTER 4

WATCH YOUR LANGUAGE

All words and attitudes of criticism are toxic. There is no such thing as constructive criticism (which is another form of self-abuse because it keeps us from connection with those with whom we desire closeness and intimacy.) When the words are "self-talk" they hold power. What we speak, our subconscious mind hears. Whatever the subconscious hears it will eventually manifest in our reality. For example, if I repeatedly affirm I'll never get a job that pays well, my subconscious will create that reality by attracting me, steering me, to low paying jobs and the internal saboteur will throw a monkey wrench into any job that disaffirms that negative belief.

Say I can't…. and I won't. Say I am… and I am. Say never…. won't ever, say always … will forever. By making can't, won't, never and always kinds of decisions, the subconscious mind hears that all alternatives, all possibility for positive alternatives, all hope, is cut off. It creates a sort of shut-down of any further use in trying. Used negatively, our "self-talk" has debilitating effects.

The words "should" and "have to" are self-defeating as well as stress producing. These are subtly intimidating in any language. "Should" and "have to" imply resistance. Going into any task or endeavor with resistance makes success just a little more difficult to attain. When the word "want to" is substituted for the word "should" or "have to" the implications are far different. By turning "should" into genuine "want to" our mind operates from the position of responsibility and control that comes from a positive attitude. The unconscious mind realizes and actualizes that position thereby creating a positive, healthy attitude toward our actions which insures success and thus produces a positive feeling.

Remember, feelings come from the inside and are validated by the world around us. Validation doesn't necessarily come directly from the recognition or praise others but does definitely come from consequences of actions; more success, more inner satisfaction, more personal growth, etc. When we look around us and the world seems just a little better for us being in it, a little cleaner, more peaceful, friendlier, safer, *that* is validation. Nice if someone notices, but not essential.

Another way that language impacts our reality is from the words we hear while growing up. Earlier you read about the effects of the significant individuals, (such as parents, relatives, teachers, clergy, etc.), various groups (girl scouts, religion, little league, t-ball, etc.), and the media (where do I begin!!!)

have had on the decisions we made about ourselves and our world. Because of the negative nature of some words we heard associated with us we internalized them, stored them and then identified with them. By becoming aware of what those words were and the meaning that we applied to ourselves, we can determine if they are working for us or not. By creating new statements about a given belief, that is, creating new affirmation, we can change beliefs on the deepest level and place them in a positive light such that life works better. We could not do this as children, but again, the task of adulthood is to empty our sand bucket and fill it with our own sand of choice.

Creating Affirmations:

Affirmations are happening all the time in our mind. We affirm beliefs merely by holding them in our thoughts. This is an example and was told to me by a colleague. A woman, I'll call her Rose (not her real name) was threatened at knifepoint by her husband and then by gunpoint shortly thereafter, endangering their small daughter, in that she was present during both events. Surely, both the mother and child were traumatized and needed psychotherapy to be able to regain a sense of confidence. However, the thoughts Rose was holding were of fear and danger. The husband was in prison but she held on to the thought that he would come and get her when he was released. She pictured the scene over and over again telling herself that in doing so she was preparing for the inevitable. Upon the guidance of a professional she was reminded that it was not inevitable, possible yes, but inevitable, no. Those negative thoughts might just be a waste of time and damaging to her physical health. It could possibly never happen. However, since there was a possibility she did need to get prepared, but not by thinking negatively about it. She needed to have some defenses in place like pepper spray, proper locks on her door, and most importantly she would take a self defense course that would empower her. Then, positive affirmations would help her shape another reality other than being a victim once again while having a plan "B" in place. So the affirmation she came up with was, "I am fully prepared to deal with any negative situation involving my husband with complete success for me and my daughter's well-being" She made it a bit smaller so she could say it 100 times a day to "I keep us safe from any harm."

Affirmations follow these guidelines:

1. Write in the present tense
2. Remain positive
3. Focus on yourself
4. Compare yourself only to yourself (this is about self-esteem, not other esteem)
5. Use action words
6. Stretch your limits
7. Proceed with workable steps.

In the accompanying workbook you will find affirmations worksheets to help you with your affirmations. Once you've created a relevant affirmation you will need to repeat it at least 100 times a day. (I do it while I'm driving the car, raking leaves, painting a wall, taking a shower, jumping on my trampoline or such relatively mindless activities.) Discipline is a choice and it takes discipline….and mindfulness but by being faithful to the practice of affirmations (as with all practices) you will soon find that these positive thoughts come into your mind every day. Trust in the power of your positive affirmations to create goodness in your life and in the lives of those you touch.

CHAPTER 5

THINKING IN PICTURES

The brain thinks in images. In the book *Life Zones*, (Corriere and McGrady, 1986), Richard Corriere and Patric M. McGrady Jr. talk about learning. They write, "I learned the answer by studying the learning techniques employed by a world-class violinist who has to learn one new composition after another. He told me that he dissects a new piece, bit by bit, learning one part after another. At some point, his brain puts all the parts together and then he has learned it. He has in his head a complete picture of the parts". The brain learns through images or pictures. To work with images is to cooperate with the brain's natural information processor. If we have an image our brain can use that image to perform many kinds of behavior, but if we know only one kind of behavior, our brain may have trouble applying the image to variable circumstances. We don't learn to take a step—we learn to walk. Walking is a series of steps. But more than that, it is an image of putting steps into action that can serve many purposes. Therefore, if our thoughts create reality and we have only one limiting thought, our reality will always be the same; but, if we have a new thought, explore new possibilities, our reality changes. If walking is all we can imagine, we will never dance, run or skate.

We don't need to know the synaptic connections of nerves to muscles and the appropriate neurotransmitter of the brain's chemistry to walk across the room or to paint a picture or drive a car. We don't need to know how the brain creates a visual image to have a visual image. The mechanism works automatically. We can simply trust our creative selves and stay out of the way. By not fretting and doubting, we can just allow life enhancing images to occur.

We visualize or "image' everything prior to acting on it. In Thomas Blakeslee's book, *The Attitude Factor*, (Blakeslee, 2005), he describes an experiment by Dr. W. Grey Walter in which electrodes were implanted in the brain of subjects at a point where the motor cortex is associated with the index finger movement. Blakeslee goes on to explain this experiment... "He amplified the electrical signal at this point and connected it to the advance mechanism on the carousel slide projector. He gave the patients the slide-advance button and told them to push it whenever they wanted to see a new slide. This was a free decision based on boredom or curiosity about the next slide. What he didn't tell them was that the button wasn't even connected. The patients were amazed to see the slides advancing just as they were about to press the button, but before they had actually made their decision to press. Their free and conscious decision to look at the next slide produced an electrical signal in their brain before they actually decided to press the button!"

Blakeslee adds that "... In our evolution from lower animals, refinements, such as language and verbal thought, were simply added on top of the existing structures which generate movement. Internal, verbal thought which evolved from speech, was a separate, later addition, not a replacement for sensory thinking. Nonverbal thinking has continued to evolve and still does the majority of the mind's work, using nonverbal knowledge directly to solve problems and generate movement."

Every action, all creativity, begins with an idea. Whether it is to get up and walk across a room or to paint a masterpiece, it begins with an idea. AS WE SET PERSONAL GOALS FOR IMPROVING OUR SELF-IMAGE AND VISUALIZE THEM, AND FOCUS ON THEM, SO WILL OUR MIND REALIZE AND ACTUALIZE THAT GOAL.

Visualization and goals:

Imagine that you are going to drive a nail into a board. Your reach for the nail and hold it at the point you intend to drive it. You reach for the hammer and hold the handle. Next you aim the hammerhead at the nail head and strike it firmly until the nail point penetrates the board. Had you never hammered a nail you would have needed to consciously think about the process and the physical mechanism would not be achieved automatically. If you were a carpenter, the process would be automatic.

Once a goal is visualized and the process understood, the mind needn't occupy itself with the physical *how* for achieving the goal.

Now, rerun this hammering process as if it were a series of stills, each tiny movement represented by one frame. The goal having been visualized, each tiny movement leading towards striking the nail head is perceived as a positive feeling. Any movement leading away from that goal is perceived as a negative feeling. The brain sends messages to the various parts of the body involved in the process without any thought at all. A sense of direction toward or away from the goal requires an adjustment on the part of the brain to correct the message. This is accomplished automatically after any visualization is made. As you continue to effect change in your life don't worry about the *how*. Allow the process to unfold while remaining aware of the goal and doing the work.

Depth perception is the same, both in actually seeing and in visualizing. To experience this, hold an object two feet from your eyes and while you fix your gaze on the object, notice the distant background. Now fix your gaze on the background and notice the object. In each case, the object not being focused on is out-of-focus. This isn't noticeable in the course of our daily seeing because we focus and refocus within split seconds to keep our entire field of vision clear. Now close your eyes and visualize an ice cream cone. See it about two feet in front of you. While keeping the ice cream cone in place, focus your vision at a point in the distance, perhaps on a person standing behind the cone and handing it to you. You may have to scan the field of inner vision by looking up and to the right with your eyes closed. Notice how the image of the ice cream cone becomes unclear. Now refocus on the ice cream cone and notice how the figure in the background becomes unclear.

Much of what we fixualize (my word, my definition: Fixating on a thought) in our mind is actually experienced in the same way, both physically and emotionally, as with an external experience. The difference between seeing and visualizing is the space in which we experience the stimuli.

The images and thoughts we hold in our mind affect the way we perceive our world as well as how our world perceives us. Sage Journal published a study in the Journal of Interpersonal Violence in which a group of men convicted of rape were shown a video of people walking down a busy street. They were asked to pick out those women whom they perceived as potential rape victims. In each case, the men picked out the same women. These women were perceived as nervous, confused or unsure of themselves. They projected a victim image. In contrast, the women who projected determination and confidence were bypassed by the study group

The images we hold of ourselves affect not only how we project ourselves and how we are perceived, but how others respond to us. An image of one's self, therefore becomes reinforced through associated feedback. Images of the self are powerful, they are real. They are created based on information received through olfactory, auditory, kinesthetic and visual data input. These data are stored in the old (limbic) brain and retrieved upon sensory stimulation. For example, it would play out this way: An individual's data bank has been filled by life experience that has been threatening, creating a self-image of a "victim". In a threatening situation the old brain is stimulated causing a similar response of being a "victim". The individual is then treated again as a victim simply reinforcing that life experience. Not only that, but the individual will also attract "bullies" to reinforce the experience which has come to be expected.

In many cases the thoughts we hold about ourselves and our world has become unconscious and habitual. While *learned* from early childhood, these thought patterns can be *relearned* to be more positive. We can become more conscious of old, negative thought patterns by becoming the observer of them non-judgmentally. As we apply new techniques and go through the processes presented here we all can begin to change negative thinking into positive thinking.

Images that result from any of life's influences, be it an image of a victim, stupid, ugly; or on the positive side, capable, confident, attractive...are the basis for decisions we make about ourselves. The image then is not who we are. It is merely an overlay of the self. It was learned and anything that has been learned can be unlearned, changed, relearned.

It is important to understand that the image does not learn, it is not influenced, it does not make decisions. Only the *self*, through awareness and learning, recognizes influence as an external force.

The *self* seeks additional information to create positive change. The *self* makes a decision to make life work, to make life feel right, to operate in harmony.

Listening to the image always keeps us where we are. The *self*, on the other hand, encourages us to take action. The healthy *self* is interested in becoming actualized. Therefore the action will always be positive.

How powerful are the images we hold in our head? Check it out. Close your eyes and bring to mind a time when you were unable to find your car keys, or purse or wallet, running late, and the misplaced item is nowhere to be found. Or imagine yourself stuck in a parking-lot-kind-of-traffic-jam, cars just not moving for more than 40 minutes. Imagine too that your are late for a critical meeting, appointment or date and your cell phone is home on the kitchen table. Take a minute or two to get in touch with that experience as if it were happening right now. Check out how your body feels. Open your eyes, take a deep breath and exhale, and as you exhale, blow away any stress and tension related to that imagined event. Again, take another deep breath and just blow away the stress. One more time, take a deep breath and as you exhale, feel the tension fall away from you. Now close your eyes again and bring to mind a time when you completed a project, a job well done, or imagine perhaps sitting by a fireplace listening to the crackle of the fire and feeling its warmth while listening to soothing music. Or imagine sitting on a quiet beach listening to the gentle surf and feeling the warmth of the sun. Take a minute or two to get in touch with the experiences. You are capable of imagining situations or events that can cause mild to extreme physical reactions within the body. Herbert Benson (Benson, 1975) addressed the benefits of positive imaging and thoughts in his descriptive work, *The Relaxation Response*. In this work he reports on the physiological effects of meditation, yoga, imagining, prayer and guided visualizations or hypnosis on such conditions as hypertension, anxiety, rage, depression, PMS, PPMS, and insomnia. The physiological changes include decreases in oxygen consumption, respiratory rate, heart rate, brain waves changes and lowered blood pressure using the various relaxation techniques.

By the way, our thoughts are not necessarily our truth. They are simply an understanding, a point of view in the present moment. Thoughts and feelings can change from moment to moment. When we are having a negative thought, holding a negative image or feeling we can check in on our *self*. We can ask; how is this thought, image or feeling serving me? What else could I choose to feel or what other thought could I hold that would serve me better. (Just a note: Here is the difference between a feeling and a thought. A feeling can be expressed in one word. If there are more words used to describe some inner event, it is a thought. For example: I feel as though I could cry... is a thought. I'm sad... is a feeling.)

CHAPTER 6

NEEDS, WANTS, DESIRES

When we navigate the waters of life with confidence we arrive at the right shores at the right time. It feels as if the activity we are involved in envelops and fills us. We feel satisfaction, energized and alert.

When we are in harmony it is like being in sync. We like ourselves, we like the feelings we are experiencing. When we are in sync we no longer spend time looking outside ourselves for those feelings. We experience success because we are at our best. It is not subject to external effect.

Being in sync occurs when we experience the moment with all our needs met. You are operating in the world without the constraints of concern for our safety or comfort.

Self-confidence, that is, a belief in the efficacy we bring to all areas of our life, is the foundation on which healthy self-image is built. In order to operate at the level of "us-at-our-best" we need to have our needs met at a level that is satisfactory to us and enables us to be on purpose. To recognize these needs is the most important step in filling them. But what are needs? And what are our needs. When we are not feeling in sync it is time to review our list of needs.

According to Dr. Abraham Maslow, (Hierarchy of Needs: A Theory of Human Motivation, Psychological Review, 1943) all human beings have a hierarchy of needs. Basic survival depends on having the first level of needs met. Further success requires that you go beyond survival and meet the needs in the second, third and fourth levels. Finally, in order to reach the ultimate goal of self-actualization and fulfillment of life's purpose, you must meet the needs of the fifth level. It is safe to say, that if your basic survival needs are not met there is little chance that you will be writing a book, going to college, or doing anything of significance; eating, breathing, keeping warm….all a first priority.

Needs are constantly changing. Life is not static. My needs as an older woman are vastly different from those as a young mother. The business executive needs someone to help do errands and get organized. The retired person needs to have errands and to explore options for relaxation, inspiration and new endeavors. However, as our environment and needs change, our *self* remains the same. If we fit into all situations with a new *self*, and an image of this new *self* comes up on the screen of our mind with every change, then we, like the clouds, have no definition. When our last child leaves home we are still the same person. When we retire from our career, we are still the same person. When we begin to have a family, graduate from school, get married, turn 50/60/70, we are still the same person. Our *self* is the basic picture with overlays of projected images that are useful at a given time, while the *self* remains intact. There is a difference between the overlay and the mask, (the mask as a presentational self as described earlier.) Perhaps one could say the overlay is transparent and the mask is more opaque.

We can be anything others expect us to be and cut off parts of ourselves for acceptance of another… or we can be ourselves. We cut parts of our *self* off when exhibiting that part becomes dangerous in our childhood experience. For example, growing up in a home where there is a lot of violence one could become invisible, so to speak, so that he or she would get out of the line of fire. Or, if every time a child made a mistake he or she was shamed, they may cut off their ability to take action. Another example would be cutting off the part of oneself that identified and expressed feelings because feelings were consistently denied and made wrong. When we cut off the parts of ourselves that we were born with, we are incomplete and look to others for completion. When we reclaim all lost parts we become ourselves knowing what we want to do and how to be. Life becomes fairly predictable and with that confidence we can navigate life with a sense of security. Imagine an ocean… and the body of water is the self and the waves are the images we project. Just as the waves constantly changing form our image is continually changing. Below the surface of the waves, the ocean, while not static, is constant. It is the constant self that allows the changing images to be healthy and appropriate.

Regardless of our early childhood experience, our self-worth, self-esteem, self-confidence and self-love can be developed, enhanced and expanded. It is merely a matter of changing our mind about ourselves and integrating those changes through self-transformation. Remember, our images do not make decisions, our mind makes decision. When we become our "true" self, we can change our image by changing our mind. And we can start by paying attention to our needs in all areas of life; in the area of work, social encounters, personal and intimate relationships. To change our mind we need to bring attention and awareness to our choices. It is all about choices.

Each situation we find ourselves in requires a choice. The question is; how do I present myself, what overlay or image is appropriate for the response I need to receive.

Imagine yourself in a new city having arrived for a business meeting. You come out of your hotel onto the street with a map of the city in your hand. Perhaps the doorman will assist you in getting a cab, perhaps the waiter will tell you where you can catch a bus to a museum, perhaps you will ask the lady at the news stand where you can purchase a local cheese or bread or wine exclusive to that area…(I think you're in France.) You will approach these people with a need and they will respond accordingly. How they respond is not personal. You will project the appropriate image by standing at least four feet away, making brief eye contact and smiling, being friendly and polite. You limit your vulnerability with these people and your needs are met. Your projected image keeps you appropriate. Are you a distant and unaffectionate person? No. Your projected image does not define your *self*.

Now imagine you have been in this city for a week and learn you will be working here for the next few months. You now have another need, the need to interact with others and to develop mutual respect and recognition with peers. You perhaps will join a group of co-workers and have dinner or play tennis on a weekend or perhaps you will join a spa or social club. Your interactions with these people will need to elicit a different response than the earlier contacts. You will have needs of belonging, respected for what you do. Your need for being active and involved will be filled when you are involved, doing something with others. The appropriate image allows you to expand your vulnerability to develop an active relationship with acquaintance. You are sociable but not intimate. Are you superficial and aloof. No. Your projected image does not define your *self*.

Imagine now that this work situation is going on much longer than you had anticipated by far. Months roll by and you begin to find that you have needs that aren't being met by strangers or acquaintances. You now begin to focus on specific people, people that you can share feeling and thought with, share similar interests and closeness. You start spending time with special people with whom you share caring and friendship. You behave with these people differently than you do with the lady at the news stand or the person you play tennis with twice a week. And be being involved somewhat more closely, you expand your vulnerability. The appropriate image you project allows you to operate apropos to changing social situations. You are warm but not intimate. Are you frigid? No, your projected images do not define your *self*.

You now have been told that this work assignment is going to be permanent. You will begin to establish roots here in this city. As you settle down you find that you have developed once again different needs. You now need to feel bonded to another person. You need to experience deep trust and unconditional acceptance and to be accepting of another. You need to be with someone with whom you can share one place in the Universe as two separate people. The appropriate image you project allows you to expand your vulnerability to allow intimate exposure.

Individuals have many different, ever-changing needs. These needs can be most suitably met when the appropriate image is presented. It isn't the image that decides but the mind. When we make up our mind about what is appropriate in any given situation we will elicit the appropriate response that fills that need.

The outcome of projecting an inappropriate image causes one to judge the outcome thereby making a decision about the *self* that is inaccurate. If to a stranger we make eye contact and stand too close and the stranger backs away, we might make the assumption that we are unlikable. If we are stiff and formal with acquaintances we socialize with and they avoid us, you might make the same assumption causing you to become shy, introverted….not who you really are.

By remaining our *self* and projecting the appropriate image, we create harmony within and all around us. You see, our image is something we create, it is an overlay, it is not the *self*, nor who we are. It can be changed. Remember, a poor self-image keeps us in the past when the actual self is living in the present.

The ability to create an appropriate overlay while maintaining the "true" *self* requires a strong sense of identity. All you need then is to know what your needs are. Read on to learn about Dr. Maslow's

Hierarchy of Needs. Dr. Maslow believed that people are motivated by needs and that needs in an ascending order must be met before going further up the hierarchal scale.

Abraham H. Maslow's Hierarchy of Needs

1. Biological and Physiological needs-air, food, drink, shelter, warmth, sex, sleep,
2. Safety needs-protection from elements, security, order, law, limits, stability.
3. Belongingness and Love needs-work group, family, affection, relationships.
4. Esteem needs-self-esteem, achievement, mastery, independence, status, prestige.
5. Cognitive needs-knowledge, meaning.
6. Aesthetic needs-appreciation and search for beauty, balance, form.
7. Self-Actualization needs – Achieving personal potential, having peak experiences.
8. Transcendence needs-helping others to achieve self actualization.

What happens when needs aren't met?

First level of needs	Biological & Psychological	Unmet
Food		Hunger
Air		Suffocation
Water		Thirst
Movement		Confinement
Freedom to explore		Restriction
Fun		Boredom
Health		Illness
Shelter and community		Homelessness
Free of physical pain		Discomfort
Rest		Exhaustion
Sex		Celibacy

Second level of needs	Safety	Unmet
Safety		Danger
Information		Doubt
Self-knowledge		Denial
Caring for others		Abandoning
Being cared for		Abandoned
Understanding		Criticism
Truth		Distrust
Financial security		Scarcity

Third level of needs	Belonging	Unmet
Friends		Loneliness
Closeness		Alienation
Sharing		Wanting
Expression of feelings		Shame
Bonding		Disconnection

Fourth level of needs	Esteem	Unmet
Love		Emptiness
Feeling attractive		Repulsion
Approval		Rejection
Respect		Scorn
Growth		Stagnation

Fifth level of needs	Cognitive	Unmet
Knowledge		Ignorance
Learning		Ennui
Exploration		Small world
Discovery		Veiled world

Sixth level of needs	Aesthetic	Unmet
Appreciation of natural beauty		Gloom
Finding pleasure in ones environment		Desolation

Seventh level of needs	Self-Actualization	Unmet
Accomplishment		Failure
Spiritual connection		Purposelessness
To be forgiven and to forgive		War

Eighth level of needs	Transcendence	Unmet
Helping others		Uselessness
Altruism		Self-serving
A higher good		Shallow existence

Each of the eight levels are driven by desire but the drives are triggered by two distinct life forces. The first four are need driven, driven by desire to survive. The last four are driven by want. They are driven by desire to create, grow, share and evolve.

CHAPTER 7

BEAUTY

William Morris, (Morris, 1880) reminds us to "Have nothing in your house that you do not know to be useful, or believe to be beautiful…" And R. Buckminster Fuller was quoted by Clifton Fadiman as saying to an engineering student, "When I am working on a problem, I never think about beauty… but when I have finished, if the solution is not beautiful I know it is wrong." What they fail to tell us, however, is the criterion for determining beauty. This is particularly important when it comes to how we see beauty in the context of our culture because within the culture beauty is often taken out of the eye of the beholder and put in a totally exterior context.

Here's another story. I came upon a newt in my kitchen. Mary Margaret, the cat, brought it in but fortunately it was unscathed by her claws and teeth. This creature is about six inches long, reddish brown in color and resembling something akin to a lizard, but with a more defined head and eyes that sit on top of the head rather than on the sides. Its legs are short and its toes are splayed… and there it stood, looking back at me. I could see it breathing through paper-thin, crepe-like skin. Assume you never saw a creature like this before (and I hadn't) and had no idea of newts being in your neighborhood. I had to decide whether to call animal control or animal rescue, maybe the police. Now I noticed that this thing lumbered rather than scooted meaning it would not be able to out run me. Having gone beyond fear and judgment, I reconsidered the previous solutions to dealing with this creature. Suddenly I experienced a transcendental moment, a realization of true beauty. I moved closer and noticed how fine its little feet were and how rich the color of the skin. I looked at its eyes and saw that it was indeed a creature of nature; living, breathing and looking right back at me. Perhaps it found me peculiar but liked my teeth or soft eyelashes (I think they call this thinking anthropomorphism, or just plain crazy.) And maybe it is looking into my eyes and praying I won't squash it. It is a moment of beauty and the beast, but who is the beauty and who is the beast? In a spirit of real appreciation of and cooperation with nature, I gently picked it up in the middle of its body, away from the grasp of its teeth (doesn't have any by the way) and carried it to a wood pile. I watch it plod to safety. With a degree of affection, I now look upon newts as "cute". That, dear reader, is the discovery of beauty.

I have another reptile story. I was sitting at my computer not long ago when I heard a thud and writhing beside me was a three foot snake with a sticky box on its head. He had fallen off the stone ledge in my office. (Sticky boxes are used to catch mice and one was left by the previous owners.

unbeknownst to me.) Not being sure the box was actually stuck to its head I feared it would free itself. So I rushed upstairs to get a broom fearing he would free himself and hide somewhere in my office in which case I would have to sell my house. Once I swept the impaired snake, who was, by the way, in no shape to resist the gentle push of the broom, through the sliding glass door onto to the deck, I could observe him fearlessly. When animal rescue came, (and yes it seemed an appropriate move to make this time around), they began to carefully un-stick the box from its head. Two capable, knowledgeable men were working at the head and about three feet down I held the other end of the snake in my hands, once again, fearlessly. Note the word fear comes up a lot. So often, fear keeps us from seeing beauty. If it doesn't look like me, sound like me, smell like me it is something to fear. At any rate, after we were done, we released the snake and I tell you, I have a whole different appreciation for snakes. They are, indeed, beautiful.

Enough about beautiful reptiles, more about beautiful humans. Beauty is the reflection of an inner experience on the outer self. It is not so much an experience of the outer world reality but a sense of inner physical, mental, emotional, and spiritual health which all comes together in a final product, a central core, which is beautiful to behold. When we walk tall, walk sexy, walk a pretty or manly walk, we can't help but feel it in the depth of our being, on a soul level. When we move as if we were beautiful we are indeed beautiful. What gives us the right? It is our birthright. We were born to manifest inherent beauty that is not judged by external criteria but rather emanates from our soul.

So what criteria can we use to determine that which is beautiful? Perhaps it is when we go beyond our fear and enter into a state of understanding; perhaps it is when we recognize that feeling of well being, safety, peace and gratitude which is inspired when gazing upon Creation, perhaps it is in accepting the experience of all living things as they naturally exist without judgment. Perhaps it is love.

So how do we define it? It is the gleam in our eyes, the warmth of our presence, the strength of our stand, the freedom of our movement that invites others to come near to learn more about us and to experience us. Beauty is not just in the eyes of the beholder, but also in how we see ourselves and the world around us. It's a choice.

CHAPTER 8

DEVELOPING POSITIVE EMOTIONS

Exploring the wounds of the past to understand the behaviors of the present is an important aspect in the journey of one's life. Extraordinary people use all the venues available and invest themselves by putting in the time and effort of self discovery without fear or hesitation as to discovering and embracing their dark side or as Jung said, the "Shadow" self.

The wounds of early childhood, ignored and denied, play themselves out in the present often as a saboteur. What this looks like is this; we put in our best effort and then it goes down the drain... all too often. Based on the negative beliefs learned early on, this failure comes to be expected. We unconsciously set it up. (Unconscious is the operative word here). After looking at the early pain and resolving it, by putting light on the dark side, we can be ready to create more positive beliefs and resulting emotions. Barbara Fredrickson (Fredrickson 2004) developed a theory of positive emotions called Broad and Build. She identified 10 aspects of our being that contribute to the manifestation of positive emotions.

1. Goal focused living – Goal focused living requires us to hold a vision of our life. This is clearly not an exercise in futurizing. What this means is living with an idea, picture or image of the bigger picture in life; my goal for old age is…. my goal for my career is…. my goal for my health is… Again, this is not an exercise in ignoring today only to plan for tomorrow. Our today is both our yesterday and our tomorrow. In my goal for good health I consider what I eat today which will help fulfill the vision of a healthy old age, how we work today will determine the fulfillment of our career vision. When we make the proper life choices today based on our goals for tomorrow we move towards that vision. Simple!

2. Character building – Strong characters are built on the affirmations of our worth. Again, language and awareness make positive traits part of the character we build. Character is often torn down by words we heard or notions that were unconsciously driven into our heads. Character building requires new ways to describe ourselves and our world, an awareness of what we bring into our consciousness, integrity and non-judgment.

3. Future mindedness – Unlike goal focused living, future mindedness involves actual planning. It calls for such habits as saving money, recycling, writing the family history, insurance,

planting seeds in the garden, etc. Future mindedness has less to do with today than it does for the future or put another way, it has to do with creating today a tomorrow that is fit for life.

4. Optimism – We may not have control of much but we do have a choice on how we see something. The glass metaphor is hackneyed at best, but it serves the purpose. Is it half full or half empty? The Universe sees all events as neutral. It is what we bring to the events, the attitudes, beliefs and such that make the experience we have. It does not serve our being or our journey to view events in a negative way. If someone I love dies I will bring to it great sadness and pain over the loss, but that is not negative. What is a negative and pessimistic aspect of such an event is to lose sight of the meaning of life and death, hang on to protracted grieving and internalize it as being necessary… the grieving takes on a life of its own beyond the loss. That is but one example of optimism vs. pessimism and a sad one at that. It is but one.

5. Persistence – Never let go of a dream. My sister told me that. Hold on to dreams that are joyful and pleasant. The dream sits in the back of the mind, coming forth when opportunity presents itself… and opportunity will present itself. Persistence also means sticking with the effort even when it becomes difficult. Pig-headedness is quiet another aspect, however. The difference is merely in the wisdom behind it. Conscious living demands we explore the difference. (A caveat: When pursuing a dream brings a negative impact on ourselves on others or on our environment, it is time to let go.)

6. Wisdom – Everyone has wisdom. It's innate. Children who are abused in the early years often do not listen to their wisdom in adulthood. They second guess it. The noise from fear of life and fear of the world we live in drowns out the words of wisdom. It is most often heard in the quiet moments, in dreams, in serendipitous moments, in meditation. Wisdom is also all around us, in children, animals, the elderly and nature. It is so present, but so overlooked if we don't listen carefully.

7. Work ethics – The work ethic is most important. What we hold as an ethic plays itself out in almost everything we do. Because we hold a certain work ethic, we require others to perform as well and tend to reward those who do as we do. For example, a work ethic can be the expectation of remuneration for our labors. Ergo, we reward others for their labors. Another work ethic might be honesty in dealings. We hold people responsible to be honest with us and we are willing to impose consequences if they do not. Therefore, we bring our integrity to our dealings and we are prepared to accept consequence if the failing is on our part. Ethics are about fairness and justice.

8. Thrift – Thrift is a character builder because it requires discipline and the ability to put off immediate gratification. Stinginess and penny pinching is quite another thing. There is wisdom around thrift that has to do with conservation of resources. Resources can be energy, both personal and global… water, food, money, oil, etc.

9. Courage – Living true to ourselves takes enormous courage. It is not taking action in the absence of fear but rather taking action in spite of danger and fear. Courage is pushing past fear.

10. Moral identity – How we define ourselves is all important to how we live our lives. Character is built on the image we hold of ourselves and others with whom we share this planet. That would be ALL sentient beings. It is a guidepost that we cannot function without and still maintain any sense of character. Of all aspects of the development of human potential, moral identity is the most determining.

When these ten aspects of personal development are paid attention to we become:

Resilient – We can remain standing in the storm and chaos that is created by those who live unconsciously. When bad things happen we can weather it, we can even grow from it.

Creative – It takes great optimism, persistence, work courage, vision and planning to create anything.

Socially integrated – Having a sense of personal strength allows one to enter into the social milieu, be it work, recreating, organization, intimacy, etc. with self confidence. Without strength of character we become chameleons in social situation, we become presentational… not authentic.

Physically healthy – Visions and goals, optimism, moral identity doesn't allow for unhealthy living. While we may get ill we are not our illness and can fully embrace the healing process with sabotaging it.

Contented – All the aspects of strong character building are based on a most important premise. That is trust. And trust involves letting go of outcomes. We do the best we can, whatever that is, with integrity and non-judgment, we rest content.

As we move through the many stages of life these positive values and beliefs carry us to achieve success and to develop resilience in the face of the challenges that walk hand and hand with success.

CHAPTER 9

DISCOVERING ONE'S SPIRITUAL JOURNEY

God
The Holy Spirit
Heavenly Father
The Source
The All
The Higher Power
Allah
Abba
Yahweh
The Divine
Jehovah
Divine Intelligence
The Creator
The Almighty

They all mean the same thing. It is reference to that which we cannot touch, cannot describe, yet most undeniably feel and experience. It is not unlike a breeze. Don't get hung up on the words, language is so limiting. In this work, that which we cannot touch nor describe will be most often be called *God or The Divine*.

Steven Hawking published *A Brief History of Time, (Hawking, 1988).* In this book he describes, in relatively simple language, the cosmological theory for the birth of the universe as a singular event happening 13.8 Billion years ago. It was a "big bang" which resulted in subatomic particles and later atoms forming stars, galaxies, planets and life as we know it.

Charles Darwin presented a startling new theory of evolution in his book *The Origin of the Species, (Darwin, 1859).* His theory caused a great deal of consternation at the time because it flew in the face of theistic evolution of the religious community. Darwin spoke of natural selection and survival of the fittest as the basis for the continuing of life on Earth.

These and many scientific theories seemed to take *The Divine* out of Creation. When we think in terms of our solar system as being one of billions in just one galaxy of billions of galaxies in this one universe we cannot help but wonder what is the force behind all this order. As science continues to explore outer space, the world beyond our world, it becomes clear that there is indeed an intelligence that we have not the words to describe. Hawking remarks in the last chapter of his book *A Brief History of Time,* that to know the source of the movement, the energy behind that which can be explained, the why of existence is to "know the mind of God". This is the God to which I refer. *The Creator, the Supreme, The Divine, Divine Intelligence, the All.*

When talking about one's "spiritual journey" it is often associated with people's personal growth over a lifetime and achieving or reaching their destiny. Along this journey, personal growth unfolds in the most individualistic and unpredictable way. It can reveal a sense of "calling" in union with *The Divine,* experiencing miracles or extraordinary experiences, even extrasensory powers. However, while such uncommon things can indeed happen, they are not the ultimate goals of the voyage. The adventure of embarking upon one's spiritual journey invites participants to explore not just the experience of The Divine in one's life, but to see the higher purpose of all experiences. The experience is extraordinary. It is nothing less than discovering the gem stored in all the graces and challenges that we live through in a lifetime and giving them meaning. As you read on, you will be reminded that spirituality involves justice, responsibility, compassion, respect, intentionality and integrity and a call to go beyond seeing *The Divine* as the good parent who gives the children protection and nurturing and unconditional love and requires only obedience to the house rules. The call is to provoke us to join the *Creator* as co-creators in a world that is sorely in need of healing. This work is transforming as it is supported with grace and is founded in the abiding love for all creation of which we, human beings, are the earthly crown.

The journey is not an easy one, it is not a high, it is not possible without fostering an ongoing relationship with *The Divine,* it is not therapy, it is not me-centered, it is not without responsibility, it is not about separation or isolation.

The term Spirituality can be understood on two levels. The first is *existential* and deals with the deepest level of action that flows out from grace. Søren Kierkegaard introduced the concept of existential spirituality in the mid 1900's in many books written by him at that time. It focused on personal, inward discoveries, rather than speculations about the supernatural. The second is *reflective* and has more to do with values, ideals, and the vision of authentic life based on doctrines. These two levels happen simultaneously. Myths, symbols and rituals found in the many traditions offer seekers the imagery and inspiration needed during this lifetime journey as well as the existential experience provides awe and depth of soul. It is both an exploration of outer space and inner space....both making the journey an adventure.

While religious events, sacred writings and ways of praying according to one's traditions support the work of spiritual awareness and responsiveness they do not in and of themselves define of the personal journey. Nor do institutions of religion define the personal experience of *The Divine.*

This quote from Shakyamuni Buddha (Gautama Siddhartha) serves as a reminder of the intimacy and singularity of one's own spiritual journey; I quote, "Do not believe on the strength of traditions even if they have been held in honor for many generations and in many places; do not believe anything because many people speak of it; do not believe on the strength of sages of old times; do not believe that which you have yourself imagined, thinking a god has inspired you. Believe nothing which depends only on the authority of your masters or of priests. After investigation, believe that which you yourself have tested and found reasonable, and which is for your good and that of others." Buddhism stresses moderation, the middle way. No right leanings, no left, but rather what is found to be reasonable and does no harm.

Three stages on the way to personal spiritual discovery:

- The first is when a person recognizes that they are uncomfortable in the choices they are making, that something is missing and that life is not working well.
- The second stage occurs when that person strives to be open to The Divine and invites guidance into their life.
- The third stage finds the person more willing to listen, to do the work and to let go of the outcomes. This is the choice of ultimate faith in the goodness of Divine Intelligence. Thus, choices are made based on the desire to fulfill ones purpose here on Earth.

This spiritual journey is a huge undertaking. Because of the vast investment one makes at this juncture, one might chose to use a teacher or mentor, often called a spiritual director, to walk with. The designation, spiritual director, is a misnomer really and might be better called facilitator, mirror, shepherd, companion, mid-wife, soul-friend who enables the soul of the seeker. It is wise to invite someone to walk with you because the process takes time and requires patience. "A good teacher accepts and celebrates where you are now, joins you in and clarifies your dreams for yourself, and helps you as a guide and adviser on the road to their attainment" Lawrence LeShan.

As with all relationships, a spiritual relationship with creation and its creator has covenants by which to abide:

- The Divine (Creator) created us and all we need to thrive. Lack is a function of our beliefs and fears that play themselves out in our world. It is not a function of Creation. It is up to us to seek the gifts awaiting us. Note: The planet we live on is fully sustainable in design.
- We have a free will, we make choices.
- We are not rescued if we choose poorly. We face consequences.
- When we realize we chose poorly and strive for wiser choices, *The Divine* supports our effort fully, unconditionally.

Spiritual journeying requires still listening and responsible action: To discern the "calling", to accept the challenge, to have a vision, to seek learning, to pray contemplatively, and meditatively and to surrender to the work.

And so it happens, at some point along the way, our journey leads us to uncover the true self, the person we were created to be, willed to be. Step by step we move from the old to the new self, from the false to the true self….step by step, slowly. The twists and turns bring us closer to the possibilities and potentials that are ours, our birthright, waiting around every corner along the way. There is always a choice and choosing isn't easy. It is willed to be but it remains our choice. It is much easier to say I had no choice, but we do….while it often is not apparent. We can be tricked into thinking there is no choice.

It takes great courage to embark upon the journey of the true self. It takes meeting the dark side of ourselves, meeting the dark side of others and bringing our light to the dark side so we can see it better. It takes willingness to make a mistake and then change. Change is always difficult and yet, "We aren't expected to be successful, but to be faithful," (Mother Teresa). We fall down, we get back up…..faithful to the work and to the journey.

The journey is to understand the demands of life. To learn to love better, to develop wisdom and compassion, to live comfortably in our skin and to define ourselves not by what we see in the mirror, not by what we are told, but by what we choose to be. Where our journey takes us is exactly where we need to be in each moment. And in those moments, if we remain awake, we have fleeting opportunities to learn and find the gem in each experience.

TOOLS FOR THE JOURNEY

Meditating:

Meditating is a daily discipline. It is a contemplative tool that you can use to withdraw into *The Divine* and to be available to the "flow" which is *The Divine* in us. Meditating provides us with an opportunity to quiet the static that constantly runs in our head. Unlike mindfulness, (a practice of being present in the moment and one I will elaborate on later), meditation involves setting aside quiet time in a quiet place. It is important to choose a time that we will be undisturbed (turn the phone off), and where we will be comfortable in a sitting posture with our spine straight. In this place we might have a small alter; a place where we are reminded of the sacredness of the practice. An alter might include a small cross, a candle, a flower, a Buddha, a religious icon or any sacred object of our tradition that touches our soul.

Twenty minutes to a half hour is an ideal amount of time to devote to a mediation session. However, in the beginning you can sit for ten minutes. We begin our meditation with a brief mindful relaxation, becoming aware of our body and breath. We begin to let go of tension quietly, gently closing our eyes, and silently repeating our mantra. A mantra is just a word or short series of words that we can go back to every time our mind begins to wander to worldly things, (as the mind is wont to do). Maranatha, Om, I am, breathe, are just a few examples of mantras.

Meditating is a discipline because it is not easy to do. Therefore, we will need to be regular and consistent in doing it every morning and every evening. It is a practice in leaving ourselves behind and being present fully in spirit to *The Divine*. In being still we are able to come alive in spirit. Meditation is centering and grounding. We are centered in our own being and grounded in *The Divine*. Letting go of all else, from this place of poverty, the spirit is awakened.

Don't worry if your mind travels to the laundry, or to the phone calls that need to be made, bills that have to be mailed, or other concerns. Just notice them and let them go returning always to your mantra and your breath. Listen to your mantra in your mind as if it were the "hum of the forest, song of the winds or roar of the ocean..." (Main, 1998) constant and reliable. Notice your breathing and relax your breathing. Just relax your body, your mind and let the thoughts go, always returning to your mantra. We enter meditation not with demands but with fidelity to the journey, in poverty, with faith, thus being free to let go and to faithfully return to our mantra.

The question often begs "why should one meditate?" The answer comes in the meditation itself but to get started a good reason, really the only reason, is to allow ourselves to be. There truly is nothing to gain, nothing to possess. In fact, it is a time to let go and go to our center where we already have everything we will ever need. Moreover it is a time for us not to need to do anything at all. As John Main, (Main, 1998), writes, "What it is about, and this is the basic aim of meditation, is to become fully aware of, fully inserted into, fully grounded in what is...it's about is-ness."

In Tibetan Buddhism there is a highly developed system of meditating consisting of five processes involving cognitive, analytical, affective, imaginal and creative processes used to explore the inner as well as the external life, and healing of the self and others. These processes are sequential and perfect the experience of meditating to the devout student. It is an advanced form of mediation and one that can be followed as the meditative practice is honed.

Meditation can bring the one who meditates to a stupendous experience of the sacred and to absolutely nothing at all. Connection and nothing are both of value. Sometimes, when thoughts invade and interfere, it is not easy to return to the mantra thus causing feelings of frustration and anxiety during the meditation. When that happens it is important to recognize those feelings, bring them to the meditation, feel them and then let them go. It is always easy to let go because the one who meditates will have mere moments before there is another opportunity to go through it again...and to once again, let go. The exercise of letting go is of value. Ergo, meditation is the experience of being *without judgment*.

Mindfulness:

Unlike meditation, mindfulness is accomplished in the noise of daily living. Life is lived in the day to day stuff and in that living is how we define our purpose. One fashions the purpose of the self through action. Thus, spirituality in the context of the whole of life can be conceived of as embodied in the human drive itself.

What we do is always by choice. Not always conscious, however. Action by conscious choice is imperative on the deepest level of spirituality. When our choices support the values and ideals Jesus taught we co-create. When we carry the message of the Tao Ti Ching and the other sacred writings in our consciousness, we make choices that support life.

So mindfulness is bringing into our awareness the very actions we are taking. It is operating in the world fully awake, taking our life off automatic pilot or off hold. So much of what we do we do unaware: driving the car, getting the mail, eating, staring at the television, preparing for bed are a mere few of the hundreds of actions we do during the day that are automatic. If we had to be present to everything we do we would probably become exhausted. Being mindful of moments during the day is like checking in on the day, seeing how our actions are supporting or not supporting our purpose. Mindfulness is a practice we can use when we are feeling un-centered to bring us back to center. As with any practice, once we have done it enough, mindfulness is readily available whenever we need it. If we are rushing through a meal mindfulness helps us to come back to the action of eating in order to appreciate the taste of the food as well as to fully utilize it in your body.

As I sit at my computer I often check out how my body is feeling. How am I sitting, does my body need me to do something different...like stretch. When I'm frazzled and rushing at the supermarket I bring my attention to exactly what I am doing...pushing the cart, reaching for a glass jar that feels cool in my hand, aware of the noise and movement around me. I become very present in my doing and thus go to my center. So it is when you step outside into the morning, or step into the shower or take out the trash. It is going to the action fully and thus to your center. It is from my center that I find connection and peace. That is mindfulness. It is bringing attention to exactly what we are doing, without judgment.

Discernment:

Discernment is ability to recognize *The Divine* moving in our life. How do we even know there is a God. Science has not been able to prove it, nor has science been able to disprove it because science is interested in quantity. *Qualia* eludes explanation. I know that when I look at a delicious apple my brain perceives it as red and I know how that works in my brain. When I see 650 electromagnetic wavelength nanometers my brain sees red, that's how it works. But, I am more than my brain. That sensual *qualia* cannot be explained by theory for once it is, it no longer is outside the realm of sensation, outside the realm of the experience of it. I cannot explain the experience of milk. It is perhaps cold, and smooth like liquid velvet and coats my tongue, a little sweet, but I cannot describe the taste of it without referring to something else that exists to compare. If I could give you an equation as to why the taste of milk is pleasurable, it would have to apply universally, and the fact is that not everyone likes milk. So too, the feeling of love for a partner is unexplainable...it just is. It is possible to say why there is love for him or her, but the quality of that love remains a mystery. Because of the awareness of the feeling, one knows love. When one feels the presence of *The Divine* in one's life it is a real experience of God, incomparable to anything else that exists and thus in the discernment of the experience, is the proof of the personal God though there may not be the words to describe it.

Discernment is the ability to tell when some decision, action or feeling is coming from a place of all good and can be recognized by the interior feelings of peace, strength of conviction and connection with others including the Divine. When a decision, action or feeling is coming from a place of evil (all bad) the interior feelings will be of confusion, anxiety, unrest, doubt, immediacy to action, and ambivalence. The interior question begs, "What's going on here?" The tools you have to help you discern are meditation and mindfulness.

In our world today we experience two opposing pulls:

- Justice in a world of exploitation.
- Frugality in a world of diminishing resources.
- Interdependence in a world of independence.
- Mutuality in a world of subordination
- Cooperation in a world of competition.
- Compassion in a world of indifference.
- Respect for diversity in a world of fear of differences.
- Global viewpoint in a world of chauvinism.

How do these pulls play themselves out in your life? Think about intimate relationships, family relationships, work, and friends. That is discernment.

Prayer:

More and more research is being done on the practice of prayer giving it more weight in healing and health. This is so partly because of the work of authors like Larry Dossy and symposiums offered to those in the healing professions. One such symposium is offered by the Harvard Medical School Department of Continuing Education and the Mind/Body Medical Institute Care Group of Beth Israel Deaconess Medical Center under the Direction of Herbert Benson, MD. and supported in part by the John Templeton Foundation. In terms of prayer the research focuses on the notion that our thoughts are consequential. What we hold in thought manifests itself in our reality. Therefore whether we speak our thoughts, or come to awareness of them, they become our prayers. Larry Dossy, in his book "Be Careful What you Pray For", (Dossy, 1996), intimates, be careful what you think about what you're thinking about. Dr. Randolph Byrd, (Byrd, 1988), published a now famous study working with patients in a coronary care unit. In a double blind study, a prayer group was randomly assigned to pray for one group of patients while these patients were matched with a control group for whom there was no prayer. There was a strong correlation between recovery and the group for who there were prayers. The most valuable aspect of these experiments on intercessory prayer is that they force us to think through very carefully, the relationship between the transcendental and worldly dimensions of our lives. By looking at praying as a non-physical event it places possibilities outside the realm of magic or voo-doo. Quantum physics enables experimenters to demonstrate nonlocal events. (Nonlocal events are those that occur outside consciousness and are non-specific to areas of the brain.)

Some points about prayer:

- There is always something to pray about.
- It allows trespasses to be brought to light. (Other's as well as our own).
- It keeps us authentic and intentional.
- Praying at night makes for nice dreams.
- It fosters self-respect through the non-judgmental quality of prayer.
- It is liberating as it helps us let go of disappointment, frustrations and anger.

Prayer can be simple. It is better when it is simple. It should be durable like weeds growing in the cracks of the sidewalk. Prayer is a river running through our lives, not a series of watering holes in a desert. Evening prayer and morning prayer time can be as short or as long as time allows. Prayer shows up in so many ways.

Prayer is in the work you do well. It is in seeing others through loving eyes. Prayer is listening. It is singing, dancing, it is original and scripture. It is being in and expressing life mindful *of The Divine's* presence without judging it. It is an offering. It is important to make time for prayer daily. Quiet or in the daily activities of living we can follow St. Paul's mandate to "Pray constantly."

Contemplation:

The root word for Contemplation in Latin is Templum which means to separate something from its environment and to put it into a domain for understanding. Contemplation is a discipline and a practice undertaken for knowledge and truth. Spiritually speaking, it is to direct the mind to an aspect of the divine and to focus on it by softening the gaze and letting the mind illuminate that which is to be learned.

Some good questions to contemplate are:

- What gives life?
- What drains life?
- For what am I most grateful?
- For what am I least grateful?
- When did I give and receive the most love?
- When did I give and receive the least love?
- When did I feel most alive?
- When did I feel the life draining out of me?
- When did I have the greatest sense of belonging to myself, to others and to the Universe?
- When did I have the least sense of belonging to myself, to others and to the Universe?
- When was I the happiest?
- When was I the saddest?
- What was my high point?
- What was my low point?

Other ponderings might be priorities in life, goals, graces, challenges and such. Keep your journal handy as you reflect all these things and spend time writing. Above all, be silent and still for it is in the silence and stillness that we hear God's response to our life.

Spiritual Retreat:

Retreats offer individuals time away to be alone for the singular purpose of contemplation. Included in a retreat may be meditation, prayer, reading, walking, and silence. Retreats can be a directed silent retreat or one that is focused on a particular issue. They can be based on a religion or incorporeal, and, for our purposes here, spiritually centered. Oftentimes it is difficult to schedule time away and/or is costly. Retreats can be made right in your own home simply by taking the phone off the hook, leaving your schedule clear for one or two days, bringing in food that is easy to prepare and healthy, and preparing your environment with music, candles, essential oils and such. Invite a friend to retreat with you honoring each others silence. Reading, walking, petting your animal and such activities enhances the peaceful feeling of a do-it-yourself retreat.

Mindbodyspirit:

There are a few requirements in having a connection with the Divine energy and one very important one is essential for the relationship to thrive and grow mentally, spiritually and physically. Developing a mindbodyspirit quality to our life calls for self/other respect, dignity and love.

What that looks like in daily life is this:

- Bring yourself in mind, body and spirit to a place of calm when stressed
- Tithe
- Nourish your body with whole foods, prepared carefully and eaten mindfully.
- Nourish the planet with awareness of its needs.
- Receive the sacraments of your traditions.
- Act kindly above all else.
- Exercise your body regularly.
- Involve yourself in issues of social justice.
- Support your family and honor them.
- Educate yourself and your children.
- Appreciate differences.

As you contemplate these goals as being affirmative and life giving you can begin to see them as options, choices in moving toward mindbodyspirit health. It is the complete opposite of abuse, either self or other.

When we take the time to meditate and spend time in contemplation, pray, discern the truth as best we can, remain mindful and practice mindbodyspirit health, the greater plan of our journey, our raison d'etre, if you will, becomes clear and we can then move forward with intention and focus. To achieve success requires that clarity and then requires a strategy to accomplish the spiritually driven goals.

PART I.... SUMMING IT UP

As we incorporate the ongoing awareness of our thoughts and take charge of what we are thinking, as we opt for positive words to describe ourselves and our world, as we make our choices based on love not fear, and use spiritual practices as we see fit, we actually begin to change our brain. We become the creators of our awesome self. Developing high self-esteem is a process and forwarding that process in a most positive and productive way requires consciousness....waking up rather than sleep walking.

Neuroplasticity is a word used to cover a broad category of brain adaptability. Yes! We can change our brain. If living with shame, guilt, anger, and uncertainty has caused low self-esteem and keeps you from achieving success, you can change the wiring that caused those beliefs. In Chapter three of Part I, you read about how the brain develops in early childhood. By the age of seven the brain is pretty much hard wired to create your world view and dictates how you will move forward in life. Now we know that we can create new neuro-pathways and thereby reinvent, recreate ourselves no matter what age. Start today!

Remember:

- Wake up

- Pay attention to feelings without judging. There is no "right/wrong/good/bad" only what works and what doesn't. Do what does.

- Focus

- Practice

- Use the tools offered in each chapter and each separate part of this book.

In the next section a strategy for success is outlined and is followed with worksheets to help you achieve you goals.

PART II

YOUR STRATEGY
FOR SUCCESS

The "law of attraction"
works for everyone
who is willing to take action.

Holding positive thoughts,
creating a mental picture
of the goal is just a first
step in achieving success.

Using a strategic plan
and following through
with action facilitates
building bridges,
climbing mountains,
fulfilling dreams or
having the love you want.

CHAPTER 1

YOUR STRATEGY FOR SUCCESS

If you never have thought about creating a plan for your life, then this will be the most important book you have ever read. If you have dreamed or wished you were wealthier or happier, could find love or inner peace, or a healthy life style but didn't know how to get it, then read on.

Let's start by exploring the law of attraction. The law of attraction states that the thoughts a person holds, the words they use, and their beliefs manifest in their reality on a physical plane. As a theory it embodies other theories such as positive thinking, prosperity theology, thought form and manifesting. Interpreting these philosophies into a single law, the law of attraction, has oversimplified very complex theories, which is misleading. Yet, to deny that positive thinking works would be, well, just wrong. It just doesn't work like magic. Stefan Klein, (Klein, 2006), science editor of a leading German newsmagazine, staff writer with Geomagazine and winner of the Georg von Holtzbrink Prize for Scientific Journalism, says in his book *The Science of Happiness*, "We should want to change ourselves rather than our circumstances." Klein also states the "… occasional efforts aren't sufficient to change our ways of perceiving. If the brain is to be rewired, repetition and habit are indispensable. And they, in turn, depend on a willingness to make an *effort*." Furthermore, there isn't a "law" of attraction, like the "law" of Gravity. A law implies that there is a fundamental principle that applies universally yet the law of attraction doesn't apply for people who don't have the resources or the advantages of creating money, cars, love, and a helicopter. It doesn't apply to those living in third world countries, or in depressed areas.

Using the theory of what the law of attraction is based on, the intention to get rich, to have more friends, to find a husband/wife/lover, or get a car, is to miss the point. It misses the point because it lacks an important element. To attain these things, we have to set goals, develop a strategy and work them. "The actual secrets of the path to happiness are determination, *effort* and time,"(The Dalai Lama, 2009).

Virtually all men and women who have achieved greatness have set goals for themselves. If you know such a person, ask them what things they think contributed most to their success. You will find goal setting is near or at the top of the list. People without goals sail a rudderless ship, whose destination depends upon the direction and force of the wind and tides, weather and other uncontrollable, external factors. And while we can't control outcomes, people without goals react to circumstances thrust upon them by life in such a way that they lose all direction. Achievement is accidental.

Professional sales people are good examples of those who find goal setting essential for success. Sales goals are typically financial ones, which are most often set by sales managers and are then required of the sales staff. These sales objectives are used to judge selling skills, to calculate commissions, raises and promotions. Sales objectives are used to compare the current sales activity to previous accomplishments, to their peers and overall professional performance in the industry. The sales goals are regularly reviewed and discussed at frequent intervals through the year to gauge whether an individual is "on track" to achieving the "numbers." The sales person is acutely aware of how he or she is doing at any given moment. This provides them with motivation to sell more, to seek and take advantage of opportunities and to modify their sales approach or practices if necessary, all the while with an eye on achieving the stated objectives. For the most part, these strategies result in sales success for everyone.

Obviously, goal setting is of value in attaining any goal, not just financial ones. Goals are vital to success at all stages of life. There is a vast amount of evidence which demonstrates the relationship of goal setting to successful outcomes for every aspect of everyone's life. Written goals are especially important. This is not surprising since all of us are used to using lists to help us accomplish tasks, or goals, such as shopping lists and "to-do" lists. With some focus and discipline most of the items on the list will have been accomplished at the end of the day. This, of course, is not accidental because these are precisely the things we set out to do.

Is achieving success or happiness less important than grocery shopping? Deciding how we want our life to turn out is the first step in making it so. Visualizing the goal and writing it down cements it in our mind. The words that follow will provide you with a guide for setting your life's goals. Using them to map out a strategy will then help you to achieve them. We know this works, and we will discuss why that is the case. BEING CLEAR ABOUT WHAT WE WANT IN LIFE, SETTING DOWN THESE OBJECTIVES, MAPPING OUR INTENTIONS, VISUALIZING THEM BY FOCUSING ON THE DESIRED OUTCOME AND TAKING ACTION CAN MAKE OUR DREAMS COME TRUE. Goal setting is essential during all stages of life, up to and including retirement. The earlier in life one learns to appreciate the value of goal setting the better, however too late to reap the rewards of reaching objectives. Happiness, contentment and success are features of living that everyone seeks and deserves regardless of age.

Elements to Success

1. Decide what we want
2. Set/write goals
3. Create a strategic plan
4. Visualize
5. Take action

All of these components are required to achieve what we want. There are really no shortcuts.

It's been said of late that the law of attraction is the secret to success. This is not a new concept. It was a tenet in Buddhism, Hinduism and written about at the turn of the century by William Atkinsen, editor of the New Thought magazine. More recently, Rhonda Byrne, (Byrne, 2006) the producer of *The Secret* maintains that you can "….close your eyes and imagine what you're wanting. The electromagnetic field of your mind goes and attracts it. The law is infallible." She fosters the notion that this, "ask, believe, receive" notion, works whether one wishes to lose weight, overcome cancer or obtain a new car. It is an integral part of achieving success.

However, just by wishing and believing you will get what you want may be more a matter of serendipity. Serendipity is the experience of discovering something of good fortune while actually looking for something else entirely. For example, I'm driving to the supermarket to buy some ice cream and there's a detour. I pass in front of a car dealership that has the exact car I've wanted and imagined and it is on the lot with a SALE sign on it. I go into the dealership and the car salesperson says that it is slashed even more because it is a demo car. I can easily afford it. I was on my way to buy ice cream...this is serendipity and it surely happens from time to time. Again, while wishing and believing is an important component to success, I wouldn't count on it happening all the time.

Most often, reaching goals takes an intention, effort, and a plan followed by *action*. Another story... Early on in my career I wanted my practice to grow large enough to totally support my lifestyle. I got the office space, had my cards printed and sat in my office waiting for clients to find me. I put out energy, prayed, visualized people filling my waiting room but indeed only a few people managed to "find" me. Then I put a marketing plan in place that included a doing a monthly mailing, attending networking meetings, presenting lectures for a small fee or no fee and putting an ad in the paper. I was consistent with my marketing plan and in six months my practice was quite healthy. The notion of "ask, believe, receive" has been challenged by serious scientists who recognize that consistent success depends both on the individual's actions and on an individual's unconscious intentions. Wishing alone cannot work except serendipitously because it calls for no action or plan of action.

A colleague commented she finds that upon taking strategic action, one's desire moves closer to fruition and then attracts more energy to that desire. She noticed that since she began to take real action towards establishing her practice there has been a chain of seemingly random events that have taken off, all of which continue to open more and more doors towards her goal. The more she works her strategy the more her intuition guides her and as she acts on her intuition, more doors open. She said it is "fascinating." Her success is exactly a result of going beyond the law of attraction, (ask, believe, receive), to include the five basic elements to achieving success; decide, set goals, create a strategic plan, visualize and take *action*.

CHAPTER 2

THE PROCESS

Decide What We Want:

The first step in reaching a goal or fulfilling a desire is to think about what we want in a particular area in our life. Since life is a process it progresses in ever changing stages. Therefore, what we want will change, morph, expand and contract as time goes by. It is important to have goals that are for the present, for the near future, and some long-range goals as well to accommodate life's process. You may notice there is a pattern or a continuum in the present, near future and long-range goals that is fairly consistent with whom we are; our values, calling and our talents. Reflect on the perceptions you hold as a "truth" in regards to the real value that goal has for your life. There are many marriages that go deeper into the power struggle when they move to the large house *of their dreams*. The wanting of it was better than the getting of it because their marriage was too frail to survive under the added stress of a big house. It is as important to get what you want as it is to want what you get so, before deciding on what it is that you are setting down as a goal, reflect on where the desire is coming from.

Set Goals in Writing:

Set your goals without regard to whether you believe they are achievable or not, and write them down. At this point don't worry too much about how you will go about achieving them. Aim high. Don't reject a goal because you don't think you are smart enough, pretty/handsome enough, clever enough, to accomplish it. Possibilities abound "outside the box." After we have decided what we really want, we will discover how true this is. You will uncover pathways to success because you have decided to do so and the waters will part for you. If you have never thought about what you'd like out of life, now is the time to think about it. A word of caution; be careful what you decide you want, because with planning, sooner or later, it is likely your goals will be realized.

In her book, *Write it Down, Make It Happen*: *Knowing What You Want and Gettting it,* Dr. Henrietta Klauser (Klauser, 2000) lists a number of books published over the years, which describe the benefit of proactive, positive thinking. She mentions Napoleon Hill's, *Think and Grow Rich,* Claude Bristol's, The Magic of Believing, James Allen's, *As a Man Thinketh,* David Schwartz's, *The Magic of Thinking Big*. The first step in all these books is to WRITE DOWN YOUR GOALS. Use the forms in this workbook and keep them where you can revisit and review them. Transpose the goal sheet (briefly) onto an index card so you can carry it in your purse, keep it on your dashboard, put it on your bathroom mirror. Look at your goal sheet and card often.

Why should writing something down make a difference? One theory is that the reticular activating system (RAS), located in the brain stem acts as a control center for filtering sensory information. Urgent information is sent to the conscious portion of your brain, while non-urgent inputs are sent to the subconscious. For example, if somebody says something we are interested in and we write it down, we'll remember it because we made it important. The RAS will filter out unrelated material and act as a sort of highlighter of relevant data.

In the same way, writing our goals down creates a sense of urgency in our brain and activates the reticular activating filter system. Deciding what we want is the first step, writing a goal out in its entirety is a second step.

Develop a Strategy:

Every successful business, every team sport requires a strategy. Landscapers, contractors, research scientists, etc. all need a strategic plan. We go to war with a strategic plan; we hopefully will come to peace with a strategic plan. A strategy helps achieve whatever the goal is.

So it is important to create a strategic plan for our goals. With each of the goals you have already decided upon, think through the sorts of things that might help you achieve them. For example, if you are seeking a life mate, you may select a variety of situations in which you would have opportunities to interact socially. Joining clubs, church groups, exploring internet dating, would be a few. If your goal is more peace in your life, it might be advantageous to relocate to a rural environment, learn yoga or mediation, or join a prayer group. These intentional situations are part of a strategy.

The more we think about our goals and strategic plan, the more likely it will be that we recognize new daily opportunities that will draw us closer to our objective. We will be more in control of our direction through these conscious and effective choices. Although many decisions may only represent small increments, they bring us ever closer to success.

Visualize:

Suppose you select a goal and then realize you have no idea how to achieve it. Do not abandon it. Visualize yourself successful in your objective. Someone once told me that the George Washington Bridge (or was it the Golden Gate Bridge???) would not have been built if it hadn't been conceived in someone's imagination. The architect had to image it first, visualize it, and see the concept of a bridge in his mind. In fact, the mind sees in pictures, not words. So, whatever the goal is, building a bridge or learning to dance, we need to see it in our mind. Then, clear pathways for right action will surface; doors open, we must take the initiative to enter; guides appear, we must seek their counsel and ask for what you need.

Take Action:

As important as it is to write goals down it is equally important that we develop a plan that depends on our own actions, not the action of external forces or other people. If our objective is the accumulation of wealth, waiting for a relative to die and leave us a fortune, or buying lottery tickets are not useful strategies because they are subject to forces outside our control. So a better strategy would be to create a budget, put some money in a bank that we choose because it has the best interest rate, to watch it grow and then to move it to another investment resource, again one we choose because it is safe. Then, when we have even more to work with we might take part of it and put it in a more aggressive investment and so on. We might also opt to spend our money more wisely in order to put more in the bank. We might pay down our debts so we aren't giving interest money to a credit card rather than to our bank account that is now growing nicely. Are specific outcomes guaranteed? Of course not. But we will see a change in the wealth we accumulate. In fact, without the plan, we would have continued to move away from the goal of wealth.

As it happens, even with the best efforts, the goal is sometimes seemingly elusive. Even with a plan we might indeed have a struggle in achieving success. Rest assured it isn't the actions that are a problem. Let me explain. Let's say you decide that part of your strategy for accumulating wealth involves finishing high school, college or obtaining specialized training, but you hold on to a thought that you don't have the money, you're too old, no time, etc. to go back to school. Consider all of those thoughts a "Saboteur" that is working very hard to keep you from getting what you want. Why would a Saboteur (that part of you that resists) do that? To keep you from getting what you want. Here's another why. Why would you not want to get what you want? It is said that the thing that we want the most out of life and don't have is the thing we are the most afraid of having. Enter the saboteur who will protect you from facing your fears. So with the above example, if all you heard growing up is that you're stupid, then going back to school might bring up such a fear of failure you just don't do it. Unconscious agendas throw roadblocks our way (such as lack of money, lack of time, being too old) so all possibilities are cut off. Night school, tutors, mentors, a connection, student loans, scholarships and other options available are not even considered. The point is that, having first decided to set our goal, we will then take action, reaching out for answers and opportunities based on a strategy that moves us in the direction of our goal. I mention the saboteur because many people are unaware of this and struggle unnecessarily. You may need to get professional help from a qualified therapist in order to identify the issues at hand and work them through so that you can proceed unencumbered.

Taking action means implementing our strategic plan. It is our actions, not those of others, upon which we will concentrate and rely. External forces may well impact our plan but challenges are there simply to be noticed and met. Keeping a picture of the end result, the accomplished goal in our mind's eye will help us to reach solutions for every challenge that comes across our path.

Sir Edmund Hillary was the first person to climb Mt. Everest and he did it at the age of 34. He did not wake up at the foot of the mountain one day and decide to take a hike. His remarkable achievement was the result of a detailed, well thought out plan, which was executed over a period of years, one step at a time. But before the plan, came the decision to do it, the goal was set, and a picture of himself at the top of the mountain was held in his mind's eye. (Academy of Achievement, 1961, Washington DC.)

There is something called "Alternate Plan B." It is perfectly fine and in fact, in some cases, a good idea to have a back-up plan to achieve the goal. Don't be afraid to modify your plan or strategy in the light of new information or circumstances to overcome obstacles and keep tracking in the direction you want. Sport teams create a "game plan" before the game based on both teams' strengths, weaknesses and proclivities. It may need to be modified throughout the game if satisfactory progress is not being made either offensively or defensively. The team members and coach keep a pulse on the progress just as you would check in with the progress you were making along the way. The goal, scoring more points than the other team, stays in view. Similarly, we can adjust our approach to achieving our goals as our environment or situation changes.

CHAPTER 3

FACTORS THAT IMPACT OUR SUCCESS OR FAILURE

External Forces:

What about luck, fate, destiny or divine intervention? Some people believe in these things and some do not. Either way, we are not meant to live our lives and our purpose merely at the whim of abstract forces. Goal setting isn't an either/or choice but moreover an essential element to success. Regardless of luck, fate, and destiny, we continue to make choices that bring us closer and in a more fruitful way to our ultimate destiny.

As discussed earlier circumstances which impinge upon our lives but which are outside our control are usually dealt with on a first-come, first-served basis. Our objective is to reach our goal in spite of adverse outside forces and allowances may be made in the strategic plan to deal with such unfavorable circumstances. If favorable, external circumstances occur to help us, so much the better.

Predetermination:

We have heard people say things like "my son/daughter was destined to become a lawyer (or priest, doctor, etc.)." Children can and often do display certain behavioral traits characteristic of certain professions, trades, and careers, and certain strengths in those same areas, which their parents and teachers recognize. These propensities are often consciously and unconsciously encouraged and it is reactions to the particular propensity which also supports them in their career pursuits. While nothing is predetermined, there are forces throughout life that impact our success or failure in the decisions we make of which we may not even be aware.

Have you heard of a "self-fulfilling prophecy?" Palm readers, Tarot card readers and seers of all persuasions often instigate self-fulfilling prophesies with each reading. Friends, family and even our own thoughts and words create self-fulfilling prophecies. It is the actualization of a previously predicted outcome manifested by unconscious thoughts and actions that support that outcome. It is a seed planted and watered in fertile soil. "This marriage isn't going to work," or "he's going to be a lawyer just like his father," or "you'll retire in Southern France" (my personal favorite) are all examples of predicted outcomes. While a self-fulfilling prophecy is often a seed planted it is manifested through an unconscious agenda in the decisions we ourselves make that manifests the prophecy.

A Dream vs. Dreaming:

Is there a difference between having a dream and being a dreamer? You bet. A dream is very often a goal, while dreaming usually involves nonspecific, amorphous thoughts. While dreaming is pleasant, unless there is planning, focus, effort and action nothing happens and nothing is the outcome. Making choices according to a plan, making sacrifices and performing hard work are elements of an action plan, not a dream state. There is a sense of intention behind the plan and whether conscious or unconscious it is a plan coupled with intention that is the force behind outcomes.

In his autobiography, Joe Theisman, (Theisman,1987), who became the quarterback for the Washington Redskins, taking them to two Super Bowls, begins his book with these words, "The boy had a dream and it was always the same. He wanted to be a pro quarterback like Bart Starr and Johnny Unitas. He took pictures out of magazines and put them up on his wall, and he would study those pictures as if there were secrets to be learned from them."

Joe's athletic skill certainly contributed to his success, but as is the case with many athletes, he worked hard at training, honing his skills and making sacrifices. Although he was tempted as a young teenager by peer pressure to "be a hood" he was afraid he would be kicked off the football team, and therefore made a behavioral choice to stay out of trouble specifically because of the goal he had set for himself. He also possessed other attributes that are often associated with goal attainment, positive thinking and visualization of the desired result. Joe says "I believed in myself. I believed I could meet any challenge."

Martin Luther King not only had a dream, a plan, a vision and a firm belief in his purpose but he surrounded himself with people who supported his goals and his actions were consistent with the direction toward which he wanted to move.

Manifesting Success:

Unless we know where we are going we will have no context in which to recognize and determine whether a specific life circumstance will help us get closer to what we hope to achieve or take us further away from it. Our goals provide the framework by which we will make daily choices. Without them we will simply bump up against life situations, react as the moment urges us and then move on to the next challenge or event. In this manner we will be waiting for things to happen to us, depending on outside forces or other people, rather than making them happen for ourselves. We will be reactive instead of proactive. When we take specific action that is part of a plan we may indeed be using collective energies of other people to make something happen, but all initiated by our own action. For example, I was 49 when I entered into my Master's program. In order to have the money for tuition I rented my house out and moved into my mother's basement apartment. I applied at a few schools and selected the one that offered the most accelerated program. I took a part time job at a mental health agency to establish myself in the community of providers and put my nose in my books. While I met a few challenges I never once took my off the goal of achieving a master degree. I used the help of many people along the way. It never occurred to me that I would not graduate at that level and I didn't see obstacles but rather solutions all along the way.

Dealing with Adversity:

We have considered the effect of external forces on our lives. On our journey we are presented with an uninterrupted supply of adverse pressures and challenges that must be dealt with and resolved as we progress. Sometimes accidents, disease, weather, wars and other disasters adversely affect our lives no matter how well we plan or set our goals. It is certainly conceivable that circumstances outside our control can derail the best-laid plan and prevent us from attaining our objectives. This is where "goal modification" comes in to the strategic plan.

Viktor Frankl, (Frankl, 2014), wrote a profoundly inspiring book called *Man's Search for Meaning*, first published in 1959. Dr. Frankl had been writing a medical manuscript almost to completion when he was forced into a concentration camp in the early 1940's. His manuscript was destroyed. Although his plan of action was drastically altered, Dr. Frankl overcame the greatest odds of ever completing it by scratching notes on scraps of paper and hiding them so that when he was released after the war ended he was able to complete his goal. The very drive to achieve his goal kept him sane and alive during that horrific period of his life and ultimately gave his life meaning.

In 2003, Bethany Hamilton, (Hamilton, 2006), then 13 years old, lost her arm to a 14' Tiger Shark while surfing off the coast in Hawaii. Three weeks after the incident, Ms. Hamilton was riding the waves and went on to be the American surfing champion, professional surfer, and winner of the 2004 ESPY Award as Comeback Athlete.

Bill Gates' first business, Traf-O-Data failed miserably, however, he states it was seminal in moving forward and becoming one of the richest people in the world. ("Interview with Bill Gates and Paul Allen", October, 1995, Fortune Magazine.)

Jim Carrey, (2000,) writes about his childhood experience in his book, *The Joker is Wild; The Trials and Triumphs of Jim Carrey*. He recounts that, at one point in his childhood his family lost their home and they for forced to live in their van. He learned the definition of poverty. His dream was to become a comedian and even in that destitute state, his father would drive him in their van to comedy clubs. At first he fell short of success but continutally got up to do it again. This happened several times before he broke through to achieving fame. Jim Carrey never let go of the dream, he did the work, and the rest is history.

To understand this a bit better I once again refer to Abraham Maslow's hierarchy of needs. He contends that the satisfaction of meeting one's "higher needs" happens only when "basic needs" are met. Referring to an earlier chapter, the "hierarchy of needs" is represented by a pyramid with the more primitive needs at the bottom of a triangle and the highest level of self-actualization at the peak. Tiered priority provides a useful reference for setting goals and knowing when to modify them to make survival possible. When we are hungry, homeless or ill, the goal of having designer shoes becomes unimportant. Food, shelter and health are the priority. That's when goal modification needs to fall in place taking priority over the previous goal in a solution oriented way.

Here's another little story. My son and his family were building their house themselves. They planned to move in July however in mid-May their son Caleb became quite ill. It took all their attention and energy to carry him through that difficult time and things did not get done on the house as planned. With their son's life on the line, the house became less important and took a back seat. When Caleb's health was secured the moving date was moved up one month and they resumed working on the house. Refocusing on a short-term problem solving goal addressed the immediate crisis while the old goal was postponed. But it was not abandoned.

Changing the Heart:

New insights and epiphanies, those life-altering moments that occur to all of us, can change a goal entirely. If your goal was to be a priest and at one point during the seminary experience you realized that this was not your calling, it is time to let go of the goal. The willingness to release a goal is important and it requires that we spend time looking at the goal, discerning its meaning to us, contemplating the shift and consciously releasing it. Releasing a goal feels very different than giving it up. Perhaps life looks vastly different, and that's okay. Sometimes dead ends provide opportunities that would not be recognized as such without the context of a set of goals in which to evaluate them. By making correct opportunistic choices and actions, it may be possible to achieve goals via a pathway entirely different from the one we initially had planned. Perhaps having a goal and strategic plan leads us to embark on a path that is an offshoot of the original one leading us to the ultimate goal in a different light. When beset by such difficult and life altering choices it is wise to talk to a therapist and spiritual director.

Thinking Positively:

In 1952, Norman Vincent Peale, (Peale, 1952), wrote a book entitled *The Power of Positive Thinking*. In it he discussed how thoughts and thought processes could affect outcomes. This is a quote from his book, *The Power of Positive Thinking*. "Any fact facing us is not as important as our attitude toward it, for that determines our success or failure. The way you think about a fact may defeat you before you ever do anything about it. You are overcome by the fact because you think you are." Norman Vincent Peale.

Dr. Peale also proposed that maintaining positive attitude could actually create favorable results while negative thinking produces failure. Although we will not attempt to restate the book contents here, every goal setter is urged to read it and incorporate Dr. Peale's principles into their lives. Again, he says, "Formulate and stamp indelibly on your mind a mental picture of yourself as succeeding. Hold this picture tenaciously. Never permit it to fade. Your mind will seek to develop the picture...Do not build up obstacles in your imagination." Norman Vincent Peale

Many of Dr. Peale's ideas have endured over more than half a century and been further validated by contemporary theorists and by physicists who have applied the complicated aspects of quantum physics to the very same notion that the thoughts we hold affect outcomes.

Persistence:

Skills and talents and vision are not enough. You may be surprised to learn that more important to successful achievement than skill is persistence. Skills mean that we have the ability to do something, not that we will. Persisting through adversity, trial and error, perhaps resetting the elements of our plan again and again will more likely bring us to our final goal. Innate ability can make the pathway easier, but only if we know what the pathway is.

PART II…. SUMMING IT UP

Be prepared to work hard, make sacrifices, avoid distractions and temptations that are not part of your goal set and which will derail or impede your strategic plan. Look for ways to stay in the right direction of the goal. What is more important, remain nonjudgmental of yourself when you stray off the path. All too often we waste precious time beating ourselves up when we make an error or make a poor choice. When we judge ourselves as stupid or in any way "bad" or wrong we impede the process of moving forward. Once again, take right/wrong/good/bad off the table and determine what is working and what isn't. Just notice it and do as the Japanese proverb says, "Fall down seven times, get up eight." Use mistakes to make better decisions in the future thereby not making that same mistake twice. Reread your goals often, study and modify your strategic plan as necessary, all the while "keeping your eyes on the prize."

WORKSHEETS

HOW TO USE THE WORKSHEETS

You are now embarking on the work portion of this adventure in success. Each worksheet provides a format for developing your values and processing your thoughts into actual goals.

SELF ANALYSIS

As you approach this adventure in success, take some time to remember who you are. This self analysis will help stimulate your thought processes about where you are headed and what you would like to achieve in life. Set aside an hour of your day to be in a place where you will be alone and undisturbed. If you come to a question that you haven't an answer for, put it off and return to it later in the day or the next day. Often answers come when we are driving the car, in the shower and falling asleep. Give this section time and space.

EVALUATING PERSONAL VALUES

In order to establish goals, it is helpful to sort out what we actually do believe in, in the various aspects of our life (our values) and how we actually live out our beliefs. Working towards the attainment of things we value will improve the quality of our life. Set another hour or two aside and go through all the aspects of your life and evaluate them without judgment. What that means is you simply notice your level of satisfaction. This exercise helps you to determine serious gaps between your how your actual life priorities correlate with your values.

YEAR-AT-A-TIME GOALS

Now you are ready to establish some goals for yourself. "Year-at-a-Time" allows you to establish short-term, mid-range and long-term goals within a distinct period of time. Some goals may be accomplished in a month or even a week. Others may take more time and some will need to be included in the following years. For example, a goal to create a garden may take years because it is a work in progress. Each year, however, it builds on itself eventually into magnificent grounds.

After writing all your goals down, rank then according to importance. Any goal that is not complete at the end of the year simply goes on to the next year's list if it is still relevant. Remember, persistence and diligence are parts of reaching your goals. If you are feeling frustration, you may need to spend some time with a friend, therapist or spiritual director to sort out your feelings and identify possible obstacles to achieving a particular goal.

STRATEGIC PLAN

Each item listed in your Year-At-A-Time worksheet needs a strategic plan sheet and number assigned to it. Indicate if it is an immediate, a near future or a long-term goal. Then write the goal clearly. After you have written it out, re-read it focusing on the purpose. Write that purpose on your strategy sheet.

Write the start date and the date you wish to target completion. How might you feel at completion? Now you can itemize the steps that lead to achieving the goal and the date of completion of each step. As you move along the year you may want to change the process. Add that to your goal sheet. Sometimes it morphs so greatly it actually becomes another goal. Start over. There is one additional page for your strategy plan. Tear it out and use it to make all the copies you need.

GOAL PROGRESS REVIEW

This is a vital report to yourself. You can use the back of the sheet to continue reporting your progress on each goal. The frequency of reviewing your progress depends a lot on the expected date of accomplishment and the complexity of the strategic process. For example, if the goal is to lose 100 pounds checking in weekly might give you a boost or a reality check in a timely fashion. If it is about building a house, perhaps because of the complexity of the project, a progress check might be best done on a monthly basis. Only you can determine that.

AFFIRMATIONS

Using your words to create positive thoughts is accomplished through the creation of an affirmation. Follow the directions on AFFIRMATIONS and complete a small, positive statement by working through the steps on the AFFIRMATION WORKSHEET.

ACKNOWLEDGE YOUR ACCOMPLISHMENTS

You did it! You accomplished your goal. Give yourself a gold star and get a massage, a beer, a cruise. Celebrate. Whether or not you achieved each and every goal 100%, or even most of them to your satisfaction, you have moved forward in your life.

If you have not accomplished your goals to your satisfaction you may experience some of the consequences of poor choices. The best-laid plans need discipline and effort. If you partied rather than studying for classes, the failure is a result of your choices. This doesn't define you, I don't care what your father said. Consequences, however, are always right behind choices and that may mean you lose your financing, have to get a job, and have to finish up your degree in a less prestigious academic institution. Fall down, face the consequences, and get back up.

ADDITIONAL READING

You will find some suggested reading at the end of the book.

SELF ANALYSIS

Take some time and think about yourself.

What are your talents? How would you like to develop them?

What are your character strengths? How can you use them for success?

What are your fears and perceived limitations? How would you overcome them?

What are your passions? How would you incorporate them in your life?

What is your work style?

What are your character or personality weaknesses? How would you change it?

What would you like to change in your personal life? In your professional life?

What would you like to change any family relationships?

Is there anything you would like to change in your environment?

What acquisitions would you like to make and when (i.e. new car, house, boat?)

What do you want to change in your neighborhood, country, and/or world?

EVALUATING PERSONAL VALUES

In each of the following areas, describe in one brief sentence, your attitudes, beliefs and feelings about that area and then follow the instructions as given in each area. Finally, circle the number to which your current actions and behaviors correlate with your beliefs on a scale of 1 (very satisfied) to 5 (very dissatisfied).

EXERCISE:
Statement: I believe exercise is...

Briefly describe a typical week of exercise.   1 2 3 4 5

HOBBIES/INTERESTS:
Statement: I believe hobbies and interests are...

Briefly indicate areas of interest and your involvement in those areas.   1 2 3 4 5

WORK/SCHOOL:
Statement: I believe work/school is...

Briefly describe your feelings about your work/course of study.   1 2 3 4 5

PERSONAL CARE:

Statement: My beliefs about personal care are...

Describe how your treat your body. Include daily grooming, professional care (i.e., haircuts, massage, chiropractors, manicures, pedicures), personal care products, etc.   1 2 3 4 5

FINANCIAL:

Statement: What I feel about money and financial security is...

Describe the relationship of money coming in, to the money going out.   1 2 3 4 5

SEX:

Statement: I feel sex is...

Describe your sexual activity over a typical month. Include degree of intimacy, number of partners, frequency of masturbation, degree of sexual satisfaction.   1 2 3 4 5

FAMILY INTERACTION:

Statement: My feelings about family are...

Describe relationships with your parents, siblings, spouse, children and extended family.   1 2 3 4 5

SOCIAL INTERACTION:
Statement: Acquaintances and friends are...

Describe your social activities and the frequency of them. Include any hobby that involves social interacting.
1 2 3 4 5

SPIRITUAL:
Statement: I feel the importance of religious or spiritual aspects of life to be...

Describe your relationship to God, a greater force than yourself, any spiritual effort including meditation, prayer, or service.
1 2 3 4 5

STRESS:
Statement: In regards to my well being I view stress as...

My level of stress is _____ (1% to 100%) most of the time. Areas of frequent stress and level:
Family   ____
Personal Relationships   ____
Health (pain/concerns   ____
Sex   ____
Finances   ____
Other   ____

In each area that you experience high stress, recall a specific example, as recently as possible, and describe it in just a few words.
1 2 3 4 5

MEDICAL CARE:
Statement: I see the importance of medical care as...

Briefly and completely describe your state of health (include pain in any area of the body, medication, conditions, number of children and physical limitations of the body as well as degree of energy.

1 2 3 4 5

When was your last physical? _____ Last dental checkup?_____
EATING PATTERNS:
Statement: I believe food to be...

Please answer the following questions briefly and as accurately as possible.

My eating pattern is (including the food, hours of the day, place and time allowed) is:
    AM: from rising...

    Mid-Day: to evening...

    PM: to bedtime

1 2 3 4 5

DRUGS AND STIMULANTS:
Statement: My feelings and beliefs about the use of drugs and stimulants are...

Indicate amounts consumed per day of:

    Caffeine   ___

    Alcohol   ___

    Tobacco   ___

    OTC drugs   ___

    Prescribed drugs   ___

    Illegal drugs   ___

Add all scores and divide them by 13. Circle that number in the sentence below:

My overall well being is reflected in the choices I make which is in keeping with my values.

                                                          1 2 3 4 5

Any area that scores a 4 or a 5 may need some fine tuning, some attention. Remember, this is not about right/wrong/good/bad. It is about what is working and what is not.

YEAR-AT-A-TIME

Life goals aren't accomplished without a plan of action.
Life goals may also take a long time to accomplish.
Life goals are milestones to reaching peace and contentment.
Life goals define the journey.
Life goals are accomplished in small steps,

The best time to begin creating a life plan-of-action is now.
Over the next year I plan to accomplish goals, feats, deeds, projects, and adventures.

Here they are: Goal/Feat/deed/project/adventure

Value   Goal

_____1._____

_____2._____

_____3._____

_____4._____

_____5._____

_____6._____

_____7._____

_____8._____

_____9._____

_____10._____

Although you may not accomplish all goals this year you will prioritize them so that the most efficacious goals will be met. Some goals might take more than a year or may even take years. You can carry unmet goals over to next year as part of the greater plan. Prioritize by placing a value to the left of the numbered item.

STRATEGY SHEET AND PROGRESS REVIEW

Create a Strategy Sheet and Progress Review for each item listed on your "Year-At-A-Time" worksheet. You can work on one goal at a time, or several, whatever feels comfortable and productive.

STRATEGY SHEET

STRATEGIC PLAN NUMBER:	DATE:

□ IMMEDIATE	□ NEAR FUTURE	□ LONG TERM

PURPOSE:

START DATE:	ACCOMPLISH DATE:	MIGHT FEEL:

STEPS TO GOAL	DATE
1.	
2.	
3.	
4.	

MORPH, EXPAND, CONTRACT (Note: Create a new goal sheet to accommodate changes if necessary)

PROGRESS REVIEW

GOAL PROGRESS AND NUMBER: DATE: _____

Am I progressing toward this objective?

If not, what got in the way or is getting in the way now, and what are the fixes or alternatives I can implement?

Are there any other actions I can think of to help me reach this objective?

What insights am I gaining as I progress?

Does the Strategic Plan need to be modified today?

Notes:

_____
_____
_____
_____
_____
_____
_____
_____
_____
_____

STRATEGY SHEET

STRATEGIC PLAN NUMBER:	DATE:

☐ IMMEDIATE	☐ NEAR FUTURE	☐ LONG TERM

PURPOSE:

START DATE:	ACCOMPLISH DATE:	MIGHT FEEL:

STEPS TO GOAL	DATE
5.	
6.	
7.	
8.	

MORPH, EXPAND, CONTRACT (Note: Create a new goal sheet to accommodate changes if necessary)

PROGRESS REVIEW

GOAL PROGRESS AND NUMBER: DATE: _____

Am I progressing toward this objective?

If not, what got in the way or is getting in the way now, and what are the fixes or alternatives I can implement?

Are there any other actions I can think of to help me reach this objective?

What insights am I gaining as I progress?

Does the Strategic Plan need to be modified today?

Notes:

_____
_____
_____
_____
_____
_____
_____
_____
_____
_____
_____

STRATEGY SHEET

STRATEGIC PLAN NUMBER:	DATE:

☐ IMMEDIATE	☐ NEAR FUTURE	☐ LONG TERM

PURPOSE:

START DATE:	ACCOMPLISH DATE:	MIGHT FEEL:

STEPS TO GOAL	DATE
1.	
2.	
3.	
4.	

MORPH, EXPAND, CONTRACT (Note: Create a new goal sheet to accommodate changes if necessary)

PROGRESS REVIEW

GOAL PROGRESS AND NUMBER: DATE: _____

Am I progressing toward this objective?

If not, what got in the way or is getting in the way now, and what are the fixes or alternatives I can implement?

Are there any other actions I can think of to help me reach this objective?

What insights am I gaining as I progress?

Does the Strategic Plan need to be modified today?

Notes:

_____
_____
_____
_____
_____
_____
_____
_____
_____
_____
_____

STRATEGY SHEET

STRATEGIC PLAN NUMBER:	DATE:

☐ IMMEDIATE	☐ NEAR FUTURE	☐ LONG TERM

PURPOSE:

START DATE:	ACCOMPLISH DATE:	MIGHT FEEL:

STEPS TO GOAL	DATE
1.	
2.	
3.	
4.	

MORPH, EXPAND, CONTRACT (Note: Create a new goal sheet to accommodate changes if necessary)

PROGRESS REVIEW

GOAL PROGRESS AND NUMBER: DATE: _____

Am I progressing toward this objective?

If not, what got in the way or is getting in the way now, and what are the fixes or alternatives I can implement?

Are there any other actions I can think of to help me reach this objective?

What insights am I gaining as I progress?

Does the Strategic Plan need to be modified today?

Notes:
_____
_____
_____
_____
_____
_____
_____
_____
_____
_____

STRATEGY SHEET

STRATEGIC PLAN NUMBER:	DATE:

☐ IMMEDIATE	☐ NEAR FUTURE	☐ LONG TERM

PURPOSE:

START DATE:	ACCOMPLISH DATE:	MIGHT FEEL:

STEPS TO GOAL	DATE
1.	
2.	
3.	
4.	

MORPH, EXPAND, CONTRACT (Note: Create a new goal sheet to accommodate changes if necessary)

PROGRESS REVIEW

GOAL PROGRESS AND NUMBER: DATE: _____

Am I progressing toward this objective?

If not, what got in the way or is getting in the way now, and what are the fixes or alternatives I can implement?

Are there any other actions I can think of to help me reach this objective?

What insights am I gaining as I progress?

Does the Strategic Plan need to be modified today?

Notes:
_____
_____
_____
_____
_____
_____
_____
_____
_____
_____
_____

STRATEGY SHEET

STRATEGIC PLAN NUMBER:	DATE:

☐ IMMEDIATE	☐ NEAR FUTURE	☐ LONG TERM

PURPOSE:

START DATE:	ACCOMPLISH DATE:	MIGHT FEEL:

STEPS TO GOAL	DATE
1.	
2.	
3.	
4.	

MORPH, EXPAND, CONTRACT (Note: Create a new goal sheet to accommodate changes if necessary)

PROGRESS REVIEW

GOAL PROGRESS AND NUMBER: DATE: _____

Am I progressing toward this objective?

If not, what got in the way or is getting in the way now, and what are the fixes or alternatives I can implement?

Are there any other actions I can think of to help me reach this objective?

What insights am I gaining as I progress?

Does the Strategic Plan need to be modified today?

Notes:

_____

_____

_____

_____

_____

_____

_____

_____

_____

_____

_____

STRATEGY SHEET

STRATEGIC PLAN NUMBER:	DATE:

☐ IMMEDIATE	☐ NEAR FUTURE	☐ LONG TERM

PURPOSE:

START DATE:	ACCOMPLISH DATE:	MIGHT FEEL:

STEPS TO GOAL	DATE
1.	
2.	
3.	
4.	

MORPH, EXPAND, CONTRACT (Note: Create a new goal sheet to accommodate changes if necessary)

PROGRESS REVIEW

GOAL PROGRESS AND NUMBER: DATE: _____

Am I progressing toward this objective?

If not, what got in the way or is getting in the way now, and what are the fixes or alternatives I can implement?

Are there any other actions I can think of to help me reach this objective?

What insights am I gaining as I progress?

Does the Strategic Plan need to be modified today?

Notes:

_____
_____
_____
_____
_____
_____
_____
_____
_____
_____

STRATEGY SHEET

STRATEGIC PLAN NUMBER:	DATE:

☐ IMMEDIATE	☐ NEAR FUTURE	☐ LONG TERM

PURPOSE:

START DATE:	ACCOMPLISH DATE:	MIGHT FEEL:

STEPS TO GOAL	DATE
1.	
2.	
3.	
4.	

MORPH, EXPAND, CONTRACT (Note: Create a new goal sheet to accommodate changes if necessary)

PROGRESS REVIEW

GOAL PROGRESS AND NUMBER: DATE: _____

Am I progressing toward this objective?

If not, what got in the way or is getting in the way now, and what are the fixes or alternatives I can implement?

Are there any other actions I can think of to help me reach this objective?

What insights am I gaining as I progress?

Does the Strategic Plan need to be modified today?

Notes:
_____
_____
_____
_____
_____
_____
_____
_____
_____
_____

STRATEGY SHEET

STRATEGIC PLAN NUMBER:	DATE:

☐ IMMEDIATE	☐ NEAR FUTURE	☐ LONG TERM

PURPOSE:

START DATE:	ACCOMPLISH DATE:	MIGHT FEEL:

STEPS TO GOAL	DATE
1.	
2.	
3.	
4.	

MORPH, EXPAND, CONTRACT (Note: Create a new goal sheet to accommodate changes if necessary)

PROGRESS REVIEW

GOAL PROGRESS AND NUMBER: DATE: _____

Am I progressing toward this objective?

If not, what got in the way or is getting in the way now, and what are the fixes or alternatives I can implement?

Are there any other actions I can think of to help me reach this objective?

What insights am I gaining as I progress?

Does the Strategic Plan need to be modified today?

Notes:

_____
_____
_____
_____
_____
_____
_____
_____
_____
_____
_____

STRATEGY SHEET

STRATEGIC PLAN NUMBER:	DATE:

☐ IMMEDIATE	☐ NEAR FUTURE	☐ LONG TERM

PURPOSE:

START DATE:	ACCOMPLISH DATE:	MIGHT FEEL:

STEPS TO GOAL	DATE
1.	
2.	
3.	
4.	

MORPH, EXPAND, CONTRACT (Note: Create a new goal sheet to accommodate changes if necessary)

PROGRESS REVIEW

GOAL PROGRESS AND NUMBER: DATE: _____

Am I progressing toward this objective?

If not, what got in the way or is getting in the way now, and what are the fixes or alternatives I can implement?

Are there any other actions I can think of to help me reach this objective?

What insights am I gaining as I progress?

Does the Strategic Plan need to be modified today?

Notes:

_____
_____
_____
_____
_____
_____
_____
_____
_____
_____
_____

STRATEGY SHEET

STRATEGIC PLAN NUMBER:	DATE:

☐ IMMEDIATE	☐ NEAR FUTURE	☐ LONG TERM

PURPOSE:

START DATE:	ACCOMPLISH DATE:	MIGHT FEEL:

STEPS TO GOAL	DATE
1.	
2.	
3.	
4.	

MORPH, EXPAND, CONTRACT (Note: Create a new goal sheet to accommodate changes if necessary)

PROGRESS REVIEW

GOAL PROGRESS AND NUMBER: DATE: _____

Am I progressing toward this objective?

If not, what got in the way or is getting in the way now, and what are the fixes or alternatives I can implement?

Are there any other actions I can think of to help me reach this objective?

What insights am I gaining as I progress?

Does the Strategic Plan need to be modified today?

Notes:

_____

_____

_____

_____

_____

_____

_____

_____

_____

_____

_____

AFFIRMATIONS

Use a blank affirmation worksheet for each area in your life in which you desire change. Write four (or more) statements that reflect WHAT YOU HAD HEARD about the ISSUE while you were growing up. Based on what you had heard, write WHAT YOU HAVE COME TO BELIEVE (it will be close to the words that you used above). In order to create a TURN AROUND write exactly what you want to create in your life regarding the issue and what qualities you possess to create that change. To place your new belief in a continuum, write a list of additional ways to substantiate your new belief. Finally, create a concise statement as your AFFIRMATION following these guidelines:

6. Write in the present tense
7. Remain positive
8. Focus on yourself
9. Compare yourself only to yourself (this is about self-esteem not other—esteem)
10. Use action words
11. Stretch your limits
12. Proceed with workable steps

Do this exercise with each area of your life you wish to change. Work on each affirmation, one at a time, in order of importance, for 21 days. Write your affirmation, put it on your mirror, dash board, and at your workplace. Even if it feels unreal to you at first, continue to repeat it at least 100 times a day until you feel like it rings true and you know it to be true. Any negative thoughts that come to mind around this affirmation also write down on a piece of paper. Acknowledge them and throw the paper away. Do this as many times as necessary while trusting in the power of your positive affirmation to create goodness in your life and in the lives of those you touch. Soon you will find that these positive thoughts come into your mind every day, with no effort on your part at all.

The following are the affirmations created by others. Perhaps they will inspire you as you create your own.
- I am smart and capable.
- I approach my fears with new confidence and strength.
- I bless my wealth and watch it grow. (My all time favorite when I had no "wealth")

AFFIRMATION WORKSHEET

THE ISSUE:

What I had heard about this issue while growing up:

1.

2.

3.

4.

Based on what I had heard about this issue in the past, I had come to believe the following about myself and my life:

A more positive belief would be:

I turn around my belief about _____ and based on my more positive belief I make the following affirmation.

AFFIRMATION WORKSHEET

THE ISSUE:

What I had heard about this issue while growing up:

1.

2.

3.

4.

Based on what I had heard about this issue in the past, I had come to believe the following about myself and my life:

A more positive belief would be:

I turn around my belief about _____ and based on my more positive belief I make the following affirmation.

AFFIRMATION WORKSHEET

THE ISSUE:

What I had heard about this issue while growing up:

   1.

   2.

   3.

   4.

Based on what I had heard about this issue in the past, I had come to believe the following about myself and my life:

A more positive belief would be:

I turn around my belief about _____ and based on my more positive belief I make the following affirmation.

AFFIRMATION WORKSHEET

THE ISSUE:

What I had heard about this issue while growing up:

1.

2.

3.

4.

Based on what I had heard about this issue in the past, I had come to believe the following about myself and my life:

A more positive belief would be:

I turn around my belief about _____ and based on my more positive belief I make the following affirmation.

AFFIRMATION WORKSHEET

THE ISSUE:

What I had heard about this issue while growing up:

1.

2.

3.

4.

Based on what I had heard about this issue in the past, I had come to believe the following about myself and my life:

A more positive belief would be:

I turn around my belief about _____ and based on my more positive belief I make the following affirmation.

PART III

A DAY IN THE LIFE OF ME

Year_____

A DAY IN THE LIFE OF ME

You're name_____

Each morning I wake to a new day filled with
all possibilities and potential.

I have the opportunity to make it magical

Whether it is in….

A smile
A touch
A kind word
A beautiful moment
A drop of rain
A kiss from the sun

There is magic available to me all day if I just keep my eyes and heart open

And each night, when I rest my head on my pillow,

I am thankful for all I was given on this day;

For love

For abundance

For a precious lesson learned

For having met my challenges with courage and Divine Grace

For all opportunities realized

And I close my eyes in gratitude.

MAKE ROOM FOR ROUTINES, MIRACLES AND MAGIC

Life happens and so does change. When our daily routine is dramatically turned upside down, or side ways, it can be quite undoing. Some of those changes are due to getting married, having children, retirement, children leaving the nest, a new job, a first job out of school, death of a spouse, moving from the city to the country-side or to another country altogether, marriage coming to an end...all of the above and more, in no particular order. Life just happens and so does change.

It is helpful to give some thought to the direction in which our life may be turning, to think about what works and what doesn't work as we make the necessary adjustments to morning routines, scheduling the day, and bringing the day to a close. It is not only helpful but also important. Living life with intention brings about the outcomes we are expecting, or at least the outcomes for which we are striving.

Life, however, is about more than routines. It is about hobbies, projects, adventures and the unexpected. When we create a plan for our life it needs to be flexible and time limited. It needs to be a reminder of what our priorities are; a reminder of the direction in which we want to head as we navigate the days, weeks, months year by year. A plan is just a reminder and guide, not a rigid set of absolutes. There is no right/wrong/good/bad in following a life plan, only what works and what doesn't work.

Keeping check on what is or is not working requires mindfulness. Mindfulness keeps us softly and gently focused. When the plan serves as a reminder of what our priorities are and a guide in direction, mindfulness brings us back to our daily living and brings us back to living in the moment. The plan then serves in partnership with intention and mindfulness in creating the life we desire in peace and joy. How do you want your day to unfold? What are the morning routines are important to get you off to a good start? What are the components that fill your day and how do you want your day to come to a close?

Our morning routine might include meditation, stretching, exercise, coffee or tea....in bed, breakfast, a run outside, quiet time spent with one's husband/wife/love discussing the day ahead or days ahead. Morning routine can be the "want –to's" of our day that are less demanding than the "have to's".

Our plan will then include the "have-to's" that keep body and soul together on this physical plane on which we live. That may be driving off to work, planting, weeding, harvesting, cleaning the house, keeping appointments, phoning, e-mails, and texts, laundry, cooking, shopping, driving home from work.

It may also include projects we would like to get to this year. That list may include repairing the broken tile, painting a room, building a deck, putting a washer in the faucet, writing that book; projects that beckon.

Through-out our lives we need adventures. Adventures may be as simple as going on a bike ride or as daring as going on a balloon ride or skydiving.

Hobbies keep our curiosity piqued. They sometimes fulfill passions or at least they stir interests that enrich life. Building a bird house may cause you to embark upon building all kinds of bird houses. Consider writing, playing the piano, gardening, sewing, golf....so many options so little time.

Why the lists. When someone asks you what is your favorite song it may be hard to come up with it because there are so many and you really haven't thought much about your favorite song. The same is true for projects, hobbies and adventures. There are so many and we often do not think about them so when we have a free day we can easily waste it with busy work.

This is your daily planner and journal. You can write thoughts, ideas, eureka moments (which happen when you are being mindful), how you intend to spend your day and finally, how you indeed did spend your day. You can add to your daily plan as you experience the changes in your life or remove any part that is not working. Your daily plan is your reminder and your guide. As you continue to use your journal you will find yourself more motivated and purposeful, accomplishing your days with more satisfaction and discovering the magic each day brings.

A MORNING PRAYER

Creator of all that is good, I now open my heart and mind to receive the gifts of joy, abundance, trust, support and compassion.

For me….

Joy is:

Abundance is:

Trust is:

Support is:

Compassion is:

AN EVENING PRAYER

Creator of all that is good,
Divine Light that rids me of my darkness,
Divine Wisdom that guides me on my path,
I know the All is available to me
And I now open my heart and mind to the gifts that carry me in joy and passion to my destiny.

I remain the willing a devoted servant to the greater good directed by Creation and Divine Intelligence.

These are my prayers. They may feel right for you…..or you can write your own. Prayers are a way of consciously communicating with Divine Intelligence/Creation in order to invite into our lives the gifts that are awaiting us and our world.

A DAILY PLANNER
AND JOURNAL

MY DAYS

Example:

My morning routine

Time

6:30	Prayer
6:45	Coffee in bed with book
7:00	Meditate
7:30	Stretch

and so on…

Now you do it

Time

Starting the day:

I consider the work I need to do on an ongoing basis:

Example:
- Laundry
- Walk the dog
- Keep appointments
- Respond to e-mails
- Return phone calls
- Clean house
- Shop for dinner

and so on....

Now you do it...
Consider the work or chores you need to do on an ongoing basis:

I usually end my day at:

In the evening I like to:

I retire for the night at:

PROJECTS:

ADVENTURES:

HOBBIES:

MY JOURNAL

Keeping a daily record of our days helps us stay on track to accomplish our projects and document our adventures so they are remembered. Thoughts, ideas and insights are woven through the journal and at the end of the year we are left with our own rich story.

Creating your journal

Keeping a journal is about the best way I can think of to track our progress as I go about creating changes in my life. A journal is more than a record of daily events and feelings. It is a to-do list, a dream book, a planner, a sketch book, a goal tracker and much more. In fact, a journal can be anything and everything that your life is about. If you were to publish your journal, it would be a best seller because it is representative of what most people feel and do.

We can organize our journal in any way that flows for us. We can create chapters of our lives giving each page a number, a date, or each chapter an age. We can index our journal by giving it chapter headings and dates.

Some of the entries for our journal could include:

> **Our dreams**...Perhaps you might write them down immediately after waking up from them or first thing in the morning. Frequently, dreams are forgotten by morning, so if writing in the dark is difficult, you might want to keep a small tape recorder by your bed and speak your dreams, then transcribe them in your journal. If a dream is hazy or forgotten, it is valuable to write the general feeling you had about the dream.

> **Our goals**...Be specific and put a time limit on achieving them. Often in writing goals specifically, we begin to question their true value to our life. This is fine. Until we are satisfied that our goal is beneficial for our life right now, we can put it on hold. Perhaps a shorter-term, smaller step to our goal would be wiser.

> **Realization of a goal**...This is our opportunity to give ourselves a pat on the back. It might be helpful to include how you feel about achieving your goal.

> **Draw**...Feelings often come up for which we have no words. Experiences that happened before we were able to speak may not be easily expressed verbally.

Cut and paste...Pictures can conjure up feelings. If you see a picture in a magazine or newspaper that you particularly like or are moved by, cut it out, paste it in your journal. Cover faces with words about the feelings.

Affirmations...In writing your affirmations, refer to your affirmation worksheet or follow the following guidelines:

1. Write in the present tense.
2. Use the pronouns I, me or myself.
3. Remain positive.
4. Focus on yourself.
5. Only compare yourself to yourself.
6. Use action words like I create, I take charge, I initiate.
7. Stretch your limits.
8. Let go of expectations of outcomes.

Inspiring quotations...Sometimes someone else says something that describes us and our feelings as if we said it ourselves.

Forgiveness...Write the names of those who hurt you and write briefly about the incidents whereby you were hurt. Then write your forgiveness to event, the act using words like, I let go of my anger, I forgive unconditionally, etc. It is important to remember that forgiveness does not condone hurtful behavior and that the offender does not have to bear consequence. It is a move towards the event such that it no longer has a hold on you and thereby freeing you from negativity so you can move forward. You need not know what forgiveness feels like. The feelings will come after the words.

Forgiveness...There's more! Write the names of those you hurt and to whom you brought pain. Again, write briefly about the incidents. Perhaps you can offer reparation. Do so if it is possible. Then, if you have done all you can to right the wrong, forgive yourself regardless of the other's ability to do so.

Go shopping in your mind...Imagine yourself in a shopping center that offers every non-tangible need for a sense of well-being with stores devoted to taking care of all your nurturing needs. Every store offers cozy, comfortable ideas for your personal care. One store offers the idea of a relaxing bath or a massage. Another is stocked with inspiration for fitness including hiking with a buddy, running on the beach, walking early in the morning. Next to that is a store that reminds you about nature by selling the idea of putting a bird feeder outside your window or a birdbath in the garden so you can watch the various birds come to visit, or puttering in the garden, and starting seedlings for Spring in the bleakness of February.

154

Buy a gift...While you're at it, make a list of special things you can do for others like sending a friend a card, makeing a phone call to a loved one just to express your love, visiting an old uncle, smiling at a stranger or reminding a stranger to smile, holding the door open for a stranger, thanking someone who doesn't expect it. Write them down.

Make a list of your blessings...all of them.

Your journal is a perfect place to put things like a loving note from a friend, a leaf, a card from a child, a "find" that you feel is save-worthy.

Your journal can also serve to record your day, the weather, your mood, or anything else that is important to you.

You can start journaling by using the journal pages in this book, part III, "A Day in the Life of Me" or if you choose to buy your journal, choose a book that catches your eye and one that you selected yourself.

MY DAILY JOURNAL

"I may not have gone where I intended to go, but I think
I have ended up where I needed to be."
Douglas Adams

"Today you are you, that is truer than true. There is no one alive who is you-er than you"
Dr. Seuss

"It does not do to dwell on dreams and forget to live."
J.K. Rowling

"Sometimes people are beautiful. Not in looks, not in what they say. Just in what they are."
Markus Zusak

"Life isn't about finding yourself. Life is about creating yourself."
George Bernard Shaw

"Life is like riding a bicycle. To keep your balance, you must keep moving."
Albert Einstein

"Some infinities are bigger than other infinities."
John Green

"Don't ask what the world needs, ask what brings you alive and go do it, because what the world needs are people who have come alive."
Howard Thurman

"There is only one happiness in this life, to love and to be loved."
George Sand

"We must let go of the life we have planned, so as to accept the one that is waiting for us."
Joseph Campbell

"Be happy for this moment. This moment is your life."
Omar Khayham

"The good life is one inspired by love and guided by knowledge."
Bertrand Russel

"God gave us the gift of life, it is up to us to give ourselves the gift of living well."
Voltaire

ABOUT THE AUTHOR

Marianne Harms, LCSW/CSW is a coach and Pennsylvania licensed psychotherapist. She has been in private practice for over 25 years in New Jersey and Pennsylvania and more recently has relocated to Sonoma to establish a couple's retreat and coaching practice in this beautiful wine country. She is a Masters in Social Work graduate of Adelphi University, New York, certified in advanced hypnosis, holds advanced certification in Imago Couple therapy and completed training in Spiritual Direction through the Center for Spirituality and Justice in New York.

Marianne has presented workshops dealing with relationship, self-esteem and spiritual awareness extensively throughout the United States. She has lectured to groups and consulted with organizations on the subject of emotional well-being through positive thinking, nutrition and exercise. Her work today is to guide and support clients in creating healthy lifestyles and relationships through understanding the dynamics of their own story, enhancing self-esteem, becoming mindful, setting goals, and working their plan. She also encourages individuals to bring spiritual and non-material awareness into their conscious choices.

Prior to her current profession, Marianne was an aesthetician and make-up artist working primarily with facially traumatized women. She worked with Stanford University Hospital Department of Plastic and Reconstructive Surgery and volunteered at the Santa Clara Hospital Burn Unit while maintaining a private studio in the San Francisco Bay area for 17 years. It was through this experience that she began to understand the effects of trauma or abuse or neglect on the psyche of an individual at any age, and how it interferes with one's ability to achieve success and fulfillment in life. Those physical scars her clients came to her with often went soul-deep and it was through this realization that she felt the impetus to move forward with her education and change gears mid-life. Answering this calling has brought much gratification to her life.

Her greatest education however came in the earlier part of her life as she struggled through her own personal challenges. Through the the guidance of a therapist and caring people, and her own belief in the ability for humans to heal even the deepest wounds, she was able to thrive and become the person she is today... positive, joyful and grateful.

More importantly, Marianne says, "Raising my sons to be happy, healthy and productive husbands and fathers is my greatest accomplishment and watching them raise their families is my most satisfying reward. I am blessed."

Marianne Harms can be reached at <u>harms.personalreflection@gmail.com.</u> She welcomes your questions and comments.

A FINAL NOTE FROM MARIANNE....

We, all of us, without exception, are trying to get to shore and we're all in the same boat. We all, without exception, will say or do something that will hurt another or we will be on the receiving end of something said or done and this happens for no other reason than getting to shore has it challenges and frail egos get in the way of our ultimate destination.

NOW, here's the important part....The only way this boat is going to make it to the shore is for love to be the driving force, the wind beneath our sails. So I, with all my faults, need to be loved by you. And you, with all your faults, need to be loved by me.... because we are love... everything else is an illusion called fear. Love is all there is.

May all you do bring you peace and joy. May your successes bring peace and joy to our world. Thank you for being the best you can be for it will be felt for generations to come.

Yours in gratitude,
Marianne

Note from the author: The second part of this book, "Your Strategy for Success" and the third part, "A Day in the Life of ME is designed to carry you through a year. You can order these two parts separately from the entire book by contacting Marianne Harms at harms.personalreflection@gmail.com for use in years to come.

RESOURCES

Agnes, Michael. *Webster's New World Dictionary,* New York: Simon and Schuster, 2003.

Allen, James. *As a Man Thinketh*, New York: Create Space Independent Thinking Publishers, 1903.

Bagdikian, Ben. *The New Media Monopoly: A completely Revised and Updated Edition with Seven New Chapters*, Massachusetts: The Beacon Press, 2004.

Bard, Dr. Randolph. The Positive Therapeutic Effects of Intercessory Prayer in a Coronary Care Unit Population, California: 2004

Benson, Dr. Herbert and Mariam Z. Klipper. *The Relaxation Response*, New York: William Morrow and Co., 1975.

Bikhchandani, Sushil and David Hirshleifer. Journal of Political Economy, Vol, 100, No. 5. A Theory of Fads, Fashins, Customs and Cultural Change as Informational Cascades, California: 1992. Last Revised 2009.

Blakeslee, Thomas. *The Attitude Factor, Extend Your Life By Changing the Way You Think, Nebraska:* iUniverse, 2005.

Book, Angela, Kimberly Costello, and Joseph Camiller. "Psychotherapy and Victim Selection: The Use of Gait as a Cue to Vulnerability". *Sage Journal* (2013): 2368 – 2383.

Bristol, Claud. *The Magic of Believing*, New York: Simon and Schuster, 1991.

Byrne, Rhonda. *The Secret*, Oregon: Beyond Words Publishing, 2006.

Carrey, James. *The Joker Is Wild: Trials and Triumphs of Jim Carrey*, New York: Firefly Books, 2000.

Corriere, Richard and Patrick McGrady. *Life Zones: A Guide to Finding Your True Self, Getting on in the Real World and Changing Losing Ways to Winning Ways*, New York: William Morrow and Company, 1986.

Dawin, Charles. *The Origin of the Species*. New York: Bantam Dell Publishing Company. 1859.

Dossy, Larry. *Be Careful What You Pray For: You Might Get it*. New York: Harper Collins Publishing Company. 1996.

E. H. Johnson. *Acts of the Buddha*. Delhi, India: Motilae Banarsidass Publishers. Ltd. 1995.

Erickson, Erik. Identity: *Youth and Crisis*. New York: W. W. Norton and Company. 1968.

Frankl, Viktor. *Man's Search for Meaning, 2014 6th Edition*. Massachusetts: Beacon Press. 1959.

Fredricson, Barbara. "The Broaden and Build Theory of Positive Emotions". Philosophical Transactions of the Royal Society B: Biological Sciences. 359 (1449): 1367–1378. 2004.

Gladwell, Malcolm. *The Tipping Point*, New York: Little Brown and Company. 2004.

Gyatso, Tenzin, *The Dali Lama of Tibet. Ancient Wisdom Modern World*, LD, EN: Little Brown & Company, New York: Little and Brown Company, 2001.

Gyatso Tenzin, The Dali Lama of Tibet and Howard C. Cutler. *The Art of Happiness*, New York: Riverhead Books. 1998.

Hamilton, Bethany. Soul Surfer: *A True Story of Faith, Family and Fighting To Get Back on the Board.* New York: Simon and Schuster, Inc., 2006.

Hawkins, David R. Power vs. Force: *The Hidden Determinants of Human Behavior,* California: Hay House. 2002.

Hawking, Stephan. *A Brief History of Time.* New York: Bantam Publishing, 1998.

Hill, Napolien. *Think and Grow Rich,* Aristeus Books, 2017.

Keyes, Ken. *The Hundredth Monkey,* Kentucky, Vision Books, 1982

Klauser, Henrietta. *Write it Down, Make it Happen.* New York : Simon & Schuster-First Fireside Edition. 2000.

Klein, Stefan. *The Science of Happiness.* New York: Marlowe & Company. 2002.

Lao-Tzu. Tao te ching (The Sacred Book of the East, Vol. 39, 1891. Translated by J. Legge).

Main, John. *Silence and Stillness in Every Season.* New York: The Contimuum-International Publishing Group. 1998.

Morris, William, *Hopes and Fears for Art: Five Lectures Delivered in Birmingham, London and Nottingham, London:* London, Ellis and White Publishing. 1881.

Peale, Norman Vincent. *Power of Positive Thinking,* NY: Simon & Schuster Fireside Ed., 2003.

Schwartz, David. *The Magic of Thinking Big,* New York: Simon & Schuster, 1959.

Swimme, Brian. *The Universe is a Green Dragon,* New Mexico: Bear & Co. Inc. 1984.

Theisman, Joseph. *Theisman,* Chicago: Contimporary Books Publishing Company, 1987.

Watson, Lyall. *Lifetide,* New York, Bantam Books, 1980.

ADDITIONAL READING

Ardagh, Arjuna. 2005. *The Translucent Revolution*, New York: The New World Library.

Gawain, Shakti. 1978. *Creative Visualization*. New York: Bantam Publishing Company.

Gladwell, Malcolm. 2005. *Blink*. New York: Little Brown and Company.

Leakey, Richard; *The Sixth Extinction*, NY: Doubleday, 1995.

Navia, Luis and Eugene Kelly; Ethics and the Search for Values, NY: Promethius Books, 1980.

Orman, Suze; *The Nine Financial Steps to Freedom*, NY: Brown Publishers, 1997.

Peale, Norman Vincent. 2003. *Power of Positive Thinking*, NY: Simon & Schuster Fireside Ed.,

Ruiz, Don Miguel; *The Mastery of Love*, CA: Ambler-Allen Publishers, 1999.

Sinetar, Marsha; *Do What You Want and the Money Will Follow*, NY: Dell Publishing, 1987

Taleb, Nassim Nicholas; *The Black Swan*, NY: Random House, 2007

Printed in the United States
By Bookmasters